BURMA

WITH SPECIAL REFERENCE TO HER RELATIONS WITH CHINA

BURMA

WITH SPECIAL REFERENCE TO HER RELATIONS WITH CHINA

BY

EDWARD HARPER PARKER,

H. M. CONSUL, KIUNGCHOW,

OFFICIATING ADVISER CHINESE AFFAIRS IN BURMA

GYAN

ISBN : 978-81-212-1521-3(HB)

First Published, 1893

Published, 2018

Published by

Gyan Publishing House
5, Ansari Road
Daryaganj, New Delhi-110002
Phone: 011-47034999, 9811692060
www.gyanbooks.com
E-mail: books@gyanbooks.com

GYAN

Printed at: G. Print Process, Delhi.

TO THE READER.

It will be at once patent to the shrewd critic that there is nothing new in this little book, which is merely a compilation from published literature. That a few of the publications here analysed are in the Chinese language, and therefore in a measure new to the reader by reason of their comparative inaccessibility, is no fault of the undersigned, who can only recommend the sceptical and the curious to furbish up their lagging Chinese and study the elegant originals themselves.

E. H. PARKER

Rangoon, March 1893.

INTRODUCTION

It is a remarkable thing that a political history of Burma, at once short, popular, and intelligible, can hardly be said to exist, notwithstanding our long occupation of the southern parts and our recent taking over of the remainder of the country. Sangermano's "Burmese Empire" is both unintelligible for want of proper and consistent dates, and incomplete, leaving out, as it does, almost entirely all account of the Chinese relations with Burma. Colonel Phayre's "History of Burma" is certainly the best hand-book on the subject, but the reader loses himself in a maze of unfamiliar proper names, often descriptive rather than personal, and the meaning of which is only intelligible to a very limited extent even to Anglo-Indians, most of whom have at least some smattering of Pali or Sanskrit to eke out their more or less perfect knowledge of this or that peninsular tongue : but even Colonel Phayre's book is not very clear as to the record of Chinese events, though these have always been amongst the most important in Burma's political history; whilst, on the other hand, the dreary and oft-repeated accounts of incessant struggles with

Aracan, Tenasserim, Pegu, Manipur, and the Shan States are unexpressibly wearisome from their sameness, and leave no very definite impression on the mind. Anderson's "Mandalay to Momein," Colonel Fytche's book of personal recollections, and Mr. James Scott's little work on Burma hardly touch upon the general political history, though Anderson's accounts, both in the popular and in the official form, are admirable so far as they go. The "British Burma Gazetteer" gives a terribly hazy and mangled account of the rise and progress of Burma : its relations with China especially are hopelessly confused. The same thing may be said of Gray's "History of Burma." A new edition of the "Gazetteer" is, however, now being prepared by Mr. James Scott, Superintendent of the Northern Shan States, and the work certainly could not have been placed in more competent hands. Bishop Bigandet's book on Gautama and his pamphlet on the "History of the Church in Burma," both of them contain some valuable historical passages. I have only just been able to get hold of Colonel Yule's "Mission to Ava", which is an academical rather than a historical work, and I have not yet had time or opportunity to read one or two old English books treating of our earlier Missions. I was given to understand by the representative of the *Missions Etrangères* at Penang that no work on Burma existed in their library there. Doubtless there must be other works of which I am ignorant, and perhaps I have inadvertently omitted to mention a few publications which I have myself read. However that may be, I never obtained anything like a clear view of Burmese political history until I began to read what the Chinese had to say upon the subject. I have now read everything Chinese that I can get hold of, and have attempted to draw up therefrom a short and, I hope, fairly clear history of Burma from the beginning, avoiding as far as possible the interlarding of all uncouth and unintelligible names, Chinese or otherwise. In the event of intelligent enquirers doubting the facts cited, I refer them to the originals, which can be purchased in Momein or Shanghai under the following not very euphonious names :—

T'êng-yüeh T'ing-chï,
Yüan Shï,
T'ang Shu,
Tung-hwa Luh,
Ying-hwan Chï-lioh,
&c., &c.

CHAPTER I.

HISTORY PRIOR TO A.D. 639.

It seems to have been quite a matter of chance that Burma should have fallen under Indian literary influence rather than Chinese, and the same may be said of Cambodgia and Siam. In any case, the chance has been unfortunate in one respect, namely, in that the Chinese aptitude for compiling careful local annals and general history has never been cultivated by any one of these three peoples. I gather from writers on Indian subjects that nearly all Indian kingdoms have also been lamentably defective in this regard, even so far as touches their own affairs, not to speak of the affairs of other states. On the other hand Annam, which from the first fell exclusively under Chinese political and literary influence, and gradually absorbed several of those Indo-Chinese states(such as Ciampa) which had been originally politically directed by Hindoo colonists, possesses almost as scrupulously exact histories as does China herself. Nothing very certain can be collected from Indian histories upon

Burma, (if I understand Colonel Phayre correctly); and Burma's own great history, the *Mahârâzâ Wen* or "Chronicle of Kings," is, as to its earlier portions, almost as valueless as the *Kojiki* or "Early History" of Japan. To add to the embarrassments of the situation, the Burmese work has not yet been fully translated into English as has been the corresponding Japanese work by Mr. Basil Hall Chamberlain; and such translated portions or digests of it as exist fail to inspire much confidence in either the sound judgment or the good faith of the compilers.

It must on a moment's reflection be evident that no history in the proper sense can possibly exist without the art of writing. There is no instance in the world of a faithful record of events, unless either the state whose events are recorded itself recorded them in writing, or unless some neighbouring state recorded the events for it. All the nations of East Asia were later than either India or China in the discovery or the borrowed use of letters, and therefore the earliest history of all such nations as Tibet, Burma, Siam, the Ailaos, Cambodgians, (who formed their alphabets on Sanskrit or Pali models); Annam, Japan, Korea, Lewchew, (who formed their script on Chinese models, with, in the case of Korea, a dash of Sanskrit); Manchuria, and Mongolia, (which formed their script first on Chinese and then on Syriac models), must be sought in the literature of either India, Turkestan, or China. Just as the Japanese "history" can be, and has conclusively been shown to be, totally untrustworthy previous to the date of the adoption or introduction of Chinese letters, so all Burmese "history" anterior to the introduction of Pali or other letters must be totally untrustworthy too. That is to say, all "history" in the one case which is not found in Chinese history, and all "history" in the other case which is not found in Indian or Chinese history belongs to the category of myth or popular tradition. In the two cases of Japan and Burma, the Chinese history of those countries is throughly sound so far as it goes. With the case of Japan, Indian history had no concern whatever; but as the Hindoo kingdoms were neglectful of their own history, it follows as of course that they would be still more neglectful of that of bordering and less civilized nations such as Burma.

We learn nothing whatever from Chinese history of any nation which can possibly be identified with the Burmese for certain until the sixth century A.D. But we have the distinctest possible statements in Chinese history that emigrants from India founded kingdoms in Sumatra, Java, Borneo, Cambodgia, and Ciampa. Therefore we may at once accept as more than probable what tradition says of the Talaings or Peguans; namely, that at a very early date they were organized into a state by missionaries and merchants from the Madras coast. Another tradition is that the Burmese, as distinct from the Peguans, who were probably a much earlier stream pouring down from the same direction, are a Mongoloid tribe emanating from the region of Tibet. The aspect and character of the modern Burmese amply supports this conjectural view, whilst the construction of their language from the point of view of etymology positively groups them with the Chinese, Kachin, Shan, Annamese branch of the human race, the chief characteristics of which are beardless faces, monosyllabic words, and tones in lieu of grammatical inflection. I know of no existing generic name for this Indo-Chinese sub-branch, which is akin to the Corean, Japanese, Manchu, and Mongolian sub-branch of the same yellow-skinned stock. Indeed the construction of Burmese from the point of view of syntax is almost identical with that of this latter sub-branch. Of Tibetan I know nothing, but I take it from inspection of the leading dictionary that there are no tones in the language, and that it savours rather of the Mongolian than of the Chinese sub-branch of the "Yellow Languages." There now remains one more radition, that Kshatriya princes from India came over *viâ* Manipur and founded the earliest Burmese state, welding into one political unit all or parts of three kindred tribes, the Pyû, the Kanran, and the Sek. This tradition is also supported by Chinese history, which first seriously mentions the Burmese (under the name Piao or Pyu) as being more or less under the influence of the Ailaos or Shans of Western Yünnan. It is added that their ancient name was *Chu-po*, a word still pronounced in some parts of China *Tüpo*, and which may without violence be compared with the T'upo or T'ufan (*i. e.* the Tibetans) of a later date. But there is nothing to prove that the Chupo were the same people as the Piao, even though found in the same region, nor did the Chinese know anything accurate about the Chupo. As to the tradition that the word Burma is derived from Brahma because the Indian state thus founded adopted that proud designation, which is supposed to be the parent of the native word Mrâmmâ or Myamma (now usually pronounced Bamma), I see nothing but pleasant fancy here, and this fancy is rudely shaken by the fact that the Kachin word for "Burmese" is "Mien" pure and simple, and that the Chinese only began to know the Burmese by the name of Mien in or about the year A. D. 1,000. All the learning in the world at present available, therefore, cannot substantiate more than this;—that the Burmese are almost certainly a Mongoloid race of immigrants from the north-west; like all other nations, welded into one from a mass of kindred tribes, one of which at least is certainly historically identified as having been called Pyû. Burmese early "history" is almost a total blank; but it can hardly be doubted that these tribes were first civilized by Hindoo immigrants; and it seems that they were first heard of in China as a nation more or less subordinate to the Ailaos or Shans, as indeed they have continued to be at various periods of their later history. Certain Shan chronicles, notably one found in recent years at Manipur, may possibly throw some small light upon the kaleidoscopic tribal shiftings between, say, B. C. 500 and A. D. 500; but, judging from those I have seen, I imagine they are all of too vague a character to be of any real historical value; and such events as seem to be in a measure capable of identification are hopelessly distorted and wrongly dated, even if they are to a limited extent true. An example is given below in connection with the State of Luh-ch'wan or Pong.

The Chinese had clearly defined relations with the Shan or Ailao Empire of (modern) Tali Fu in the first century of our era, and in A. D. 90 one Yung Yu, King of T'an, sent tribute to China through the good offices of the Ailao, receiving an official seal from China. The Chinese seem to take it for granted that Yung Yu of T'an was of the same race as a later Pyû king named Yung K'iang. In A. D. 220-230 the celebrated Chinese warrior K'ung Ming or Chu-koh Liang undoubtedly carried his arms as far as Yung-ch'ang, if not up to T'eng-yüeh or Momein, but China was then split up into three kingdoms, and Chu-koh Liang's master's kingdom in modern Sz-ch'wan can hardly be called "China," nor is there any complete, history of it and its foreign relations such as there is of the other two, both of which were much more considerable as political factors in the Eastern world.

The Ailaos were next called Nanchao when they re-appeared upon the Chinese political stage. There can be no question of identification, for the Annamese still call the Laos of Upper Siam by the name Ailao, and the Chinese tell us that Nanchao was the "southern" or *nan* of the six *chao* or "princes," adding that *chao* was a barbarian word for "prince," which it still is in Shan, Laos, and Siamese. Nanchao we are told bordered on Magadha, which quite explains how the Kshatriya princes could find their way by at least one route to Burma. To the south-west of the Nanchao were the Piao (still pronounced Pyu in Cantonese, which is the best Chinese representative dialect). During the 8th century the T'upo (usually now called T'ufan) or Tibetans struggled with China for mastery over Nanchao, and the Nanchao king Kolofung annexed both the Pyu and also part of Assam. It is from this time only that trustworthy Burmese history can be said to begin, just as génuine Japanese history begins in the 4th or 5th century, when relations with China had become constant. From this period India may be said to disappear as a political factor from Burmese history.

On the whole I am disposed to think that the visits of King Yung Yu's envoys between the years A.D. 97 and A.D. 120 may be left out of consideration so far as touches the history of Burma. It is known from the Chinese annals that merchants or envoys from some part of the Roman Empire came to China during the second century of our era by way of Indo-China, and from the account given in the Chinese histories of T'an State, it seems not unlikely that this State really lay much further west than Burma, and was only originally known to China because its envoys approached China through Burma and Yünnan. The only connecting link between King Yung Yu of T'an and the kings of Pyu is that both bore what the Chinese call the "family name" of Yung; and Alompra, whose name was Yung Tsih-ya or Aungzeya, in 1,750 is stated to have claimed descent from the kings of T'an and Pyû in a letter which he wrote to China; or, what is much more likely, the Chinese translators concocted the genealogy for him. It is altogether absurd to suppose that an illiterate villager like Alompra could have been accurately versed in a 1,700 years' course of Burmo-Chinese history, when we see now that the most erudite Burmans have the merest smattering of comparative or general historical knowledge, and that their own history utterly disfigures the few Chinese names which tradition has handed down. Besides, the later Chinese have always imagined that the Burmese word *Maung* ("brother" or "Mr.") is the family name of most Burmans, and the same thing *mutatis mutandis* with other "barbarous" nations.*

The utmost that can possibly be extracted from Colonel Phayre's history is that a chief of the Pyû named Thamuddarît, not directly descended from the legendary Kshatriya kings of Tagaung, in the

* I remember being once much puzzled by the following poem (here of course translated) by a Chinese Minister to England. "Mi-sz, her small name was Anna; one of the beauties of all ages, T'a-ma-sun." It was simply a "Miss Anna Thompson" who had captivated his excellency, and had her "family name" of Mi-sz and her other names thus travestied.

second century A. D. founded a new dynasty at Pagan. The vaguely mentioned Chu-po and T'an of early Chinese history may or may not be remotely connected with the equally vague Kshatriya kings: there is no advantage in pushing the speculation failing further evidence. All that Colonel Phayre really has to say for certain of Burmese history up to the date of the establishment of the "common era" in A. D. 639 may be compressed into one line:—during this period Buddhism, introduced from some place or other, more or less successfully struggled with the previously existing superstition, character uncertain.

CHAPTER II.

THE DAWN OF TRUE HISTORY.

We are now on safe ground, and have reached a point where Chinese and Indo-Burmese histories meet. The Javanese (*i.e.* the emissaries of Hindu kingdoms in Java) who visited China said that the Piao or Pyû called themselves Dulichu (or some such word), and that their territory was bounded by Cambodgia, East India, Yünnan, and the sea. Evidently therefore the Burmese or Pyû State must have been nearly as extensive then as it was first found in our own days. The names of 18 dependent States, nine walled cities, and 32 out of 298 districts are given, but it is not possible to identify a single one with any certainty. Perhaps Moh-Yin and Alikih may be identified with the modern Mo-hnyin (or Mêng-yang as the Chinese call it) and Aracan. The king's title was *Mo-lo-jê,* which the well-known rules of phonetic interchange enable us to say for almost a certainty is intended to represent the sound *Ma-râ-jâ.* This is all the more likely in that the king's minister was called *Mo-ho-si-no,* the first part of the double word evidently also being *Mahâ.* I now proceed to translate from the Chinese :—

"When the king of the Piao goes out in his palankoen, he reposes on a couch of golden cord; but for long distances he rides an elephant. He has several hundred female attendants. The circular wall of his city is built of greenish glazed tiles, and is 160 *li* (over 50 miles) in circuit.It has twelve gates, and there are pagodas at each of the four corners. The people all live inside it. Their house tiles are of lead and zinc, and they use the wood of the *Nephelium lichi* as timber. They dislike taking life. They greet each other by embracing the arm with the hand. They know how to make astronomical calculations, and are devotees of Buddhism. They have a hundred monasteries, with bricks of vitreous ware, embellished with gold and silver vermilion, gay colours, and red kino. The floor is painted and covered with ornamented carpets. The king's residence is in like style. The people cut their hair at seven years of age, and enter a monastery. If at the age of twenty they have not grasped the doctrine, they become lay people again. For clothes they use a cotton *sarang*, holding that, as silk cloth involves the taking of life, it ought not to be worn. On the head they wear golden-flowered hats with a blue net or bag set with pearls. In the king's palace there are placed two bells, one of gold and one of silver; when an enemy comes they burn incense and beat the bells, in order to divine their good or évil fortune. There is a huge white elephant a hundred feet high: litigants burn incense and kneel before the elephant, reflecting within themselves whether they are right or wrong, after which they retire. When there is any disaster or plague, the king also kneels down in front of the elephant and blames himself.*

"They have no manacles, and criminals are flogged on the back with five bamboos bound together, receiving five blows for heavy, and three for light offences. Homicide is punished with death. The land is suitable for pulse, rice, and the millet-like grains. Sugarcane grows as thick as a man's shin. There is no hemp or wheat. Gold and silver are used as money, the shape of which is crescent-like: it is called *têng-k'a-t'o* and also *tsuh-t'an-t'o.* They have no grease or oil, and they use wax and various scents instead for lighting. In trading with the neighbouring states of their class, they use porpoise [? skin], cotton, and glass jars as barter. The women twist their hair high up on the crown of the head, and ornament it with strings of pearls; they wear a natural-tinted female petticoat, and throw pieces of delicate silk

* Some accounts say "image" instead of "elephant," the two words being identical in sound.

over themselves. When walking, they hold a fan, and the wives of exalted persons have four or five individuals at each side holding fans. Near the city there are hills of sand and a barren waste which also borders on Po-sz and P'o-lo-mên, and is twenty days from the city of Si-shê-li. The Si-shê-li of the Buddhist classics is Central India.

" Nan-chao used to exercise a suzerainty over it on account of its contiguity and by reason of the military strength of Nan-chao. Towards the close of the eighth century A. D., the King Yung K'iang, hearing that Nan-chao had become part of the T'ang* Empire, had a desire to join China too, and Imousün sent an envoy named Yang Kia-ming to Kien-nan. The Viceroy of Si-ch'wan, Wei Kao, begged permission to offer the emperor some barbarian songs, and moreover told the Piao State to send up some musicians. For specimens of their music see the General Annals. His Majesty Divus Têh made Shu-nan-do President of the Imperial Mews, and sent him back. The Governor of K'ai Chou submitted a panegyric upon the Piao music.

"In the year 832 the Nan-chao monarch kidnapped 3,000 Burmans and colonised his newly acquired eastern dominions with them."

---

* That is the empire of the Chinese ruling house of T'ang.

All the above is from the chapter on "Southern Barbarians" in the T'ang history. Governor Sü Ki-yü's Geography adds that the Piao music brought to China was all in the *fan*(*i.e. vam, bam, or brahm*) dialect; that is, Sanskrit.

It will be at once evident that a great deal of this descriptive account exactly corresponds with the Burma of our time: the golden couch, the elephants, the dislike of taking animal life, devotion to Buddhism, numerous temples, temporary embracing by all youths of the monastic discipline, use of the *sarang* or *lun-dji*, use of the *denga* (still the Burmese word for coined money, *do* being the Burmese sign of the plural), twisting up and ornamenting the hair, style of female dress, &c. &c., all point unmistakably to well known Burmese characteristics of to-day. Imousün was the most in evidence if not the most distinguished of the Nanchao kings. Kien-nan and K'ai-chou were both in Sz-ch'wan, or Si-ch'wan, as part of it was then called. Shunando we are told elsewhere was the king's heir, and, as *nandaw* means "palace" in modern Burmese, it seems not improbable that there may be some attempt in the trisyllabic word to translate the Chinese words *tung-kung* or "eastern palace," meaning "heir-apparent." Governor Sü Ki-yü's Geography states that the envoy on this occasion was one Sih-li-i, the king's younger brother, so that it is all the more likely that *Shunando* is not a personal name. Chinese history tells us that Imousün's father annexed the dominions of the Pyû, and that his son styled himself *Piao-sin.* This word suggests the Burmese *Pyû-sheng* or "King of the Pyû," just as some of the modern kings styled themselves *Hseng-byu-sheng* or "lords of the white elephant." Any way, it is abundantly clear that during the ninth century Burma, whatever its size may have been, was, at least so far as its northern portion was concerned, inferior in power to the Shan kingdom of modern Tali-Fu, which at one time came very nearly overthrowing the Chinese T'ang dynasty.

The Burmese computation of time being essentially Hindu, we may at once accept Colonel Phayre's suggestion that the reformation of the calendar and installation of the common era was Hindu handiwork too. Indeed at this time China herself was under the influence of and was alternately accepting and persecuting Buddhist and Hindoo ideas.

CHAPTER III.

THE DEVELOPMENT OF MEDIAEVAL BURMA.

During the 5th century the Northern Wei Tartar dynasty of China both re-introduced Buddhism on a large scale, and also introduced a new calendar invented by a man of Northern Liang, a powerful semi-Chinese state bordering on Turkestan, which afterwards became a great artistic and religious centre. But still nothing tangible can be predicated of Burmese history,— at least nothing so tangible as what we find recorded of the Pyu in Chinese history,– until the rise of Anawrat'â, who was consecrated as king in A. D. 1,010. There is another significant work by a Chinese writer called Fan Ch'oh on the subject of the southern barbarians. It differs but slightly so far as Burma is concerned from the T'ang historian's account, but it states explicitly that communication "with the Pyu state," which was 79 journeys south of Yung-ch'ang, were opened by the Nanchao King Kolofung. When the Chinese speak thus, they invariably mean the "centre or capital" of a state. Colonel Yule alludes to this peculiarity when Marco Polo speaks of the "City of Mien." The early history of Pegu is almost a complete blank, all records having disappeared in the incessant wars with Burma; but it may safely be assumed, especially in view of the Chinese statement that the Pyu territory extended to the sea, that the Talaings or Peguans and the Pyu or Burmans alternately had the upperhand, as they continued to do indeed after the conquest of Pegu by Anawrat'â. As Colonel Yule remarks with his usual sagacity:—"One cannot but have some suspicion that "the desire to carry back to a remoter epoch the exist- "ence of the empire as a great monarchy has led to "the representation of what was really the history of "various petty principalities, attaining probably an "alternate preponderance of dominion, as the history "of one dynasty of monarchs in various successive "seats." All that Colonel Phayre can infer is that Brahmins and Buddhists contended for mastery, and that the country during the 8th century was perpetually disturbed by religious troubles. From that time to the close of the 13th century the native annals of Pegu are, to use his own words, almost a blank.

It seems rather a barren result, but it would appear undoubtedly a fact that, traditions apart, (and what savages have not traditions ?), Burmese history, whether of north or south Burma, up to the beginning of the eleventh century consists of what is given above, and no more. Nor is there any thing existing in the country to suggest very much in addition. There is no accumulation of wealth, there are no permanent buildings except the interminable useless bricked-up Buddhist pagodas: no royal tombs: no municipal traditions: no really ancient inscriptions, and what old religious inscriptions there are seem generally to be utterly devoid of historical interest: no literature worth the time involved in reading it (Gray considers that the Burmese obtained their letters from the Talaings in the 10th century) : in short, the country is just as much a barren waste from a civilised and civilising point of view as the steppes of Mongolia: generation after generation of its aimless people have gone and come in the same listless way as the Tartar nomads, for all the world like so many butterflies or sheep, the death-rate being the highest known in any part of the of world, owing to the shiftless neglect of parental cares. I may here quote another of Colonel Yule's shrewd generalisations:—" There is a deep "element of barbarism in the Burmese character, but "looking to Pagan and other evidences, it may be doubt- "ed whether their civilization, such as it is, was not "fully greater eight centuries ago than in later days."

Anawarat'â, then, was the first definite king of Burmese history, and he reigned at Pagan, (spelt in Burmese Pugân). Accordingly we find one century later a statement in the Chinese Sung dynasty's history that in the year A. D. 1,106, the P'u-kan State brought tribute: this would be during the reign of Anawrat'â's grandson Alungsîthu, and leaves a space of 100 years within which Burma may be presumed to have thoroughly made the acquaintance of China, which is reasonable enough. *Two* Burmese states sent tribute between the years 1,127 and 1,163, a fact which militates once more against the assumption of unified dominion.

Anawrat'â seems to have been an ardent Buddhist, and to have made raids upon "the false Arîs," much in the same way that China did upon the Taoists, Nestorians, and other rival sects. Whatever the competing state of Pegu may have once been, it was politically annihilated and incorporated, together with all its religious paraphernalia, by King Anawrat'â of Pagan. The fragmentary Talaing chronicle still existing, which consists chiefly of a bare tale of half-fabulous kings, fifty-one in number, confirms this important event in a few vague sentences of lamentation. Anawrat'â, prompted no less by ambition than "by religious zeal," is now supposed to have marched into Gandalarît (a name applied by the Burmese chronicle to a part of Yünnan) in order to secure the holy tooth said to have been preserved in China. There is nothing at all unlikely in this. Holy teeth were now a drug in the Chinese market, and during the 7th century a Brahman (or a native of the Indian state called *Polomên* or *Brahman* by the Chinese) arrived at the Chinese metropolis of Si-ngan Fu with a Buddha's tooth. The Nestorian priest Olopên arrived about the same time. Persecution of both Buddhism and Taoism was now going on, but notwithstanding this, in the year A.D. 615 there were 100,000 Buddhist priests and nuns in China. During the 9th century the well-known Chinese statesman Han Yü got into trouble for protesting against the worship of Buddhist *shari, sariri,* or relics. All this about Anawrat'â is therefore very credible. But when Colonel Phayre goes on to say:—"The "Emperor of China at first took no notice of the King. "At length they had a friendly meeting. Anawrat'â "failed to obtain the relic he sought, but brought away "a golden image which had been sanctified by direct "contact with the holy tooth,"—we must protest. Indeed Colonel Phayre himself in a way points out that the independent state of Nanchao must really be meant, and not China. I say "in a way" because he leaves us to infer that the Sung dynasty had reincorporated Nanchao after the decaying T'ang dynasty had let it slip. The fact is the first Emperor of the Sung dynasty in the middle of the 10th century "drew a line," beyond which he was determined to have no political concern, and the Nanchao state, now first called the Kingdom of Tali, was quite independent up to the time of the Mongol inroad under Prince Kublai, afterwards Kublai Khan.

Prince Hassan of Rangoon, son of the ill-fated Panthay "Sultan" Tu Wên-siu, informs me that the *P'eh-tsz* or *P'u-tsz* tribe in Yünnan are the descendants of the ancient Nanchao people; but though this may be the case, it seems that the Chinese histories also give to them the same name (*Peh-i* or *Pai-i*) as is given to the Shans. Prince Hassan insists that the languages of the two stocks differ; but as he is not very learned in Chinese literature, owing to his long absence from China, and as the wisest Chinese have no idea whatever of comparative philology, least of all of "barbarian" languages, I think we must accept without demur the overwhelming existing evidence that the Ailaos and Nanchaos are the race progenitors of the Shans, Laos, and Siamese of to-day, though possibly the *P'eh-tsz* branch of that race may have once exclusively held the reins of political power. I also think the Shan "Kingdom of Pong" which Anawrat'â enumerated amongst his conquests must have been the native half of the Nanchao empire after its disintegration, as distinct from the Chinese half ruled over by the semi-Chinese Twan dynasty of Ta-li Fu. I also think that the "Kingdom of Pong," as Pemberton's Manipur chronicle calls it, must have covered ever varying parts of the area now represented by the *sawbwa*ships of Mogaung (Mêng-kung), Mo-hnyin (Mêng-yang), and perhaps Momeit (Mêng-mih) and North Theinni (Muh-pang), and also by several mediatised Shan states now forming part of the Chinese dominions, such as Nan-tien, Kan-ngai, Lung-ch'wan, Mêng-mao, Man-mu or Man-moh, Hulasa, &c., &c., &c.

The name *Mien* as signifying Burma only became known to the Chinese about this time, and they themselves state so. Those who accept the Burman theory that this word is identical with the Burmese word *Myan-ma*, *Mrâm-mâ*, or *Brahm-ma* do not seem to me to have a good case to defend. When the modern Burmans want to say "Brahman," they they *Pounna*, and if they had desired to keep up the idea that they were Brahmans by origin, it is difficult to see why they should go out of their way to coin a new word out of one and the same parent original, and thus obscure their own aim. The Kachins, who seem to be a cognate race with the Burmans, call the Burmans *Mien*; but whether the Chinese got this name from the Kachins or the Kachins from the Chinese it is difficult to hazard an opinion, as the Kachin immigration has only in comparatively recent years displaced that of the older Shans. Yet there is nothing extraordinary about this uncertainty. Why and when were the Russians first called Russ? Why do the Burmese call the Chinese *Taroup* or *Tayouk*? At least one half of the world's national designations will perhaps be found to be inexplicable except by vague tradition. What seems certain is that the leading Burmese people were known to the Chinese by their old tribal name of Pyu until A. D. 1,000 at least, and that the Burmese claim to a great antiquity for the name Mien or Myan is probably like many other things Burmese, a piece of empty, anachronous, and bombastic pride, and no more reasonable than would be the derivation of the word "English" from "angels."

After the reign of Alaungsithu, Arakan was brought into closer relation with the Pagan monarchy. It must not be forgotten that the Arakan branch of the Mrâmmâ race claims to be the elder, just as the Shans of Laos claim to be the elder branch of the Thai race. If there had been any truth in the Brahman theory, it is pretty certain that the elder branch would also call themselves Mâramâ (their form of Myamma or Bamma) instead of "natives of Rakhaing-pyi" or Rakhaing-land. I cannot discern any ground whatever for supposing with Colonel Phayre, (quoted by Colonel Yule) that the Kanran were the Aracanese. There are two places at least called Kan-lan by the Chinese, so that if there is any justification for speculation at all, the evidence, such as it is, points east rather than west. Aracan has never had any relations with China. Neither has Pegu; that is Pegu considered as being a distinct state from Pyu, Pagan, and Mien; nor has Manipur, though the Chinese have records of the existence of both Aracanese and Manipurese peoples under the name *A-li-kih* and *Kieh-sie*, this last name being an imitation of the word Cassè or Cathay, meaning "Manipur-people." The Shans had possession of these two kingdoms at different times, and for several centuries incessant fighting seems to have gone on between the rival Shan and Burmese kingdoms of Pong, as the Manipureans called the one, and Mien, as the Chinese call the other. Pong never seems to have had any relations with imperial China until the arrival of the Mongols on the scene. In fact, China was completely shut out from all communication with Magadha, Manipur, Aracan, and Burma by the semi-independent Chinese-Shan kingdom of Tali, which itself went by various names during this unsettled period. All these countries were consequently more or less subjected to Indian and Buddhist influences, and consequently we find that all without exception use alphabets based on Pali or Sanskrit, to the utter exclusion of the Chinese character. Burmese history during this period of transition is barren and wearisome, and very few prominent features can be laid hold of to indicate a steady development in the scale of civilization. Not an invention, not an art, science, or book of wisdom ; no public works, no improvements, a dead level of priestly mendicancy and totally useless but expensive pagodas, coupled with complete absence of material home refinement and social luxury. According to Gray the first poem written in the Burmese idiom was composed in A. D. 1,453, and it appears from Colonel Yule's account of the Pagan inscriptions that so recently as 200 years ago the square character was in use and not the round one as at present in vogue.

CHAPTER IV.

THE MONGOLS AND BURMA.

The Mongols knew nothing whatever of Mien except that parts of it were conterminous with Tali. In the year A. D. 1,242 they shewed signs of threatening the state of Tali, then still under the kings of the Twan family. Kublai himself conquered the state in 1,254 and placed the king's minister in charge of it as the king's *süan-fu-shï* or "Conciliator," leaving to him the duty also of conquering the neighbouring tribes. The above events took place during the reigns of Gayuk and Mangu Khans. Kublai succeeded Mangu in A. D. 1,260. Amongst the other "Conciliators" was that of Luh-ch'wan, probably the Chinese name for the Shan kingdom of Pong, for many Pong events and names described in the Manipur chronicles tally, except as to date, with similar events and names described in the Chinese chronicles of Luh-ch'wan, which state then included the present Chinese *sawbwa*ships of Lung-ch'wan and Mêng-mao at least, if not more. The only other Chinese protected *sawbwa*ship which dates from 1,260 is that of Kan-ngai, or Kan-ngeh as the

Mongol History writes it. Both these states were subordinate to the Mongol Military Governor of Kin-ch'ï or "Golden Teeth," generally and probably rightly considered to be the Zardandan of Marco Polo. The modern Burmese-protected Shan *sawbwa*ship of North Theinni, called Mêng-pang or Muh-pang by the Chinese, also submitted to the Mongols, who passed through it on their road to attack Annam. As Mêng-pang is the Chinese form of the Shan *Muong-Pang* or "the Pang State," it becomes a question whether the "Pong State" of the Manipur chronicle did not rather refer to Theinni, which originally included Mêng-mih or Momeit. Be that as it may, during Kublai's reign the whole of the Shan *sawbwa*ships included between Manipur and Annam were at least nominally subject to the Mongol dynasty of China.

In the year 1,271 the *süan-wei-sz* or Mongol Comforter-in-chief of the Shan provinces sent a messenger to Mien or Burma to demand tribute. This man is called "*K'ih-tai* T'oh-yin" in the Mongol Annals, and perhaps the first part of this name may be the latter part of Colonel Phayre's "Uriang *Kadai*" a man who is supposed to have compelled the recognition by Burma of Mongol power is 1,256. Neither the Burmese nor the Chinese Annals say anything about any collision at this date, but the Mongol messenger returned from his mission with a Burman envoy named Kiai-poh in his charge. The Mongol history says nothing about the demand for tribute having been based on the precedent of Anawrat'â's having sent gold and silver vessels. As we have seen, Anawrat'â never could have reached China at all; moreover the Chinese, who always carefully chronicle such facts, make absolutely no mention of Burma during the period of Anawrat'â's existence. Nor is there any need to suggest such a ground for the demand, as the Mongol claim to the world's tribute was universal. In 1,273 Kublai Khan wrote a letter to Burma reminding the king that Kiai-poh had been to Peking, and had been allowed to inspect certain Buddhist relics; also requesting that some persons of the royal blood should be sent up to go through the usual tributary forms. War was hinted at in case of refusal. This allusion to the relics certainly suggests some kind of connection, in the Burmese mind at least, between Anawrat'â's earlier demand on the state of Tali for such, and China's present exhibition of them in this case: but that has nothing to do with what passed in the Chinese or Mongol mind, or with the suggestion that

China based her demand on Anawrat'â's precedent. A report came in 1,275 from the Mongol or Chinese Governor in those parts to the effect that one of the Golden Teeth chiefs had been punished by the Burmese for shewing K'ih-tai T'oh-yin the way to Burma. This chief also informed the Mongols that there were three roads to Burma, all uniting at Kiang-t'ou *ch'êng*, or "River Head" city, a place which must have been near modern Bhamo. He offered the assistance of certain of the Burmese Shan *sawbwas.* Matters were hastened on to a crisis by the additional fact that some of the Mongol emissaries were being detained by the Burmese. Still, Kublai declined to declare war just then.

But in the year 1,277 the Burmese attacked Kan-ngeh (between Bhamo and Momein or T'êng-yüeh), and even threatened to establish a post between this last place and Yungch'ang Fu (Marco Polo's Vociam). The Mongol chiliarch of Tali, aided by one of the Twan family rulers, (who was now reduced to the status of military governor under the Mongols), travelled with all speed to meet the Burmans, who are said to have numbered between 40,000 and 50,000 men, having with them besides 10,000 horses and 100 elephants. The Mongol general had only 700 men, but with this small force he completely routed the enemy in a series of encounters upon the Tapeng River, somewhere between Nantien and Kan-ngeh. Colonel Phayre, who follows the Burmese account, makes out that the latter were "overpowered by numbers :" this, however, is probably mere Burmese bluster, for, whatever the Chinese faults, it must be confessed that their histories are fair and accurate, whilst, whatever the Burmese virtues, it must be admitted that their histories are full of inaccuracies and braggadocio. Later on in the same year, Nah-su-lah-ting (Nas'reddin) marched with over 3,800 men, partly Mongols and partly men of the various Yünnan tribes, straight upon Burma. He reached Kiang-t'ou city, but was compelled to return to China on account of the excessive heat.

Nothing seems to have been done from now until the year 1,283, when Nas'reddin undertook a campaign with 10,000 Sz-ch'wan Chinese troops and the few Mongols already on the spot. One column, taking 200 boats with them, marched by the ordinary Manwaing route, the other by way of Lung-ch'wan, the two meeting at Kiang-t'ou city, which place they took by storm. There can be little doubt that Kiang-t'ou city must be Colonel Phayre's Ngatshaungyan, which he places south of Bhamo, for the fact of Burmese defeat and the dates agree in both histories. Neither the Chinese name nor the Burmese name seems to be now in use.

Colonel Phayre says the inhabitants of Pagan were in confusion and terror, and that the king abandoned the city, which was entered and plundered by the Mongols. That the Burmese should run away is quite in accordance with what we know of Burmese style of conducting war, but the more sober account of the Chinese is probably the true one, as the Chinese themselves are not given to minimising their victories. According to the Mongol History, the King of Burma sent an envoy craving for pardon, and a Mongol ambassador named K'ieh-lieh was sent to arrange terms. This was in 1,285. Colonel Phayre says that some arrangement seems to have been made, but that no details are recorded. Neither does the Mongol history explain why in the following year, 1,286, another army was ordered to march upon Burma; but it may safely be assumed that certain of the Mongol emissaries were murdered at this time; and, as the Mongol history makes no mention of previous murders, we may reject Colonel Phayre's version, taken from the Burmese history, that it was the

distinct statement that "the Prince of Yünnan "marched upon Pagan, losing over 7,000 men in do-"ing so;" and Governor Sü Ki-yü's geography says that "Comforters of Pang-ya and other places were established at the Royal Burmese city of Pagan." On the other hand certain passages in Colonel Yule's book point to a like confusion in other matters between old and new Pagan. There is no such discrepancy of seven years as Colonel Phayre supposes to exist between the Chinese and the Burmese dates. Moreover, when Marco Polo says that Nas'reddin defeated the Burmese on the "plain of Vociam," he is quite right, as the Golden Teeth territories, including Nantien and Kan-ngai, were and are still part of Yung-ch'ang Fu, for the T'êng-yüeh or Momein department or sub-prefecture was only removed to its present site 250 years ago. Colonel Phayre is mistaken when he says:—"according "to the histories of both countries there was only one "great pitched battle," for we have seen that there were two, and we have also seen that Nas'reddin won the second and not the first, so that Marco Polo is the sole author of the supposed confusion in either case.

Why the Burmese describe the Mongol armies as consisting of two races, the Tarouk (written Taroup) and Taret it is impossible to conjecture. Colonel Phayre says the Manchus are by the Burmese called Taret, and it is hardly necessary to tell Burmese students that the Chinese are now all called Taroup (pronounced Tayouk.) Colonel Phayre's suggestion that Tarouk is probably "Turk" cannot be sustained. The very name of *T'uh-küeh* or *Durkö* had disappeared from the current Chinese language by this time, having only been in popular use from A.D. 500 to A.D. 1,000; and there is no reasonable similarity, to be accounted for on any etymological hypothesis, between the sounds *T'uh-küeh* and *Taroup,* both of which, again, are written in a way which leaves us to merely guess what the respective pronunciations might have been 600 years ago. Besides, what did the Burmese call the Chinese before the Mongols came? There were certainly no Manchus in the Mongol army, for none of the Tungusic races (of which the Manchus formed a small tribe) are anywhere supposed to have fought for their enemies the Mongols, who had only just crushed them; and the word Manchu, the meaning of which has never yet been satisfactorily explained,* was un-

* I have since writing the above come upon a partial explanation given by the Manchu (*i.e.* Chinese) emperor K'ien-lung, but it is of no importance in connection with the subject under criticism. I also observed that Colonel Yule gives the Manipur words for "six" and "seven" as *taruk* and *tarel,* which is really an extraordinary coincidence.

known until the 17th century A. D. We may therefore reject all these theories as being unsupported speculations, and say that the origin of the words Mien, Taroup, Taret, and Manchu belongs to the category of the quite unknown. On the other hand, the word *Siam* is a barbarous Anglicism derived from the Portuguese or Italian word Sciam, this last being an attempt to represent in Italo-Portuguese fashion the Burmese imperfect nasal sound *Shan* (written *Sham*) applied by them to the whole Tai or Thai group of people, and itself again of doubtful meaning.

To sum up therefore. Chinese accounts of the Pyu begin long before the existence of any such state as Pong or of any other Shan principalities is alluded to in any history or chronicle, and always in connection with the Shan empire of Nanchao. No other neighbouring states are mentioned except Magadha, Tibet, and Annam. The Nanchao empire splits up, and China proper is for many centuries entirely cut off from Magadha, Burma, and the Shans, the state (probably Chinese-Shan) of Tali standing between as an impenetrable obstacle. The various Shan tribes which once formed part of the Nanchao empire, evidently unable to stand against Chinese thrift and industry, are either absorbed and become Chinese subjects, or migrate and gradually form the states of Laos, Luang Prabang, Vienchan, Zimmé, and Siam, as they have in our own day been called. Others nearer to their old home mix up in Assamese and Manipur politics, for a time even rule those states, and form the palatinates (ever changing) of Mogaung, Mamu, Mêng-pang, and Luh-ch'wan. These Shan or Thai races struggle with Mien and with the Ta-laing or Burmo-Peguan races, and the result is that after the events above recorded we find the Shans actually in possession of Burma. Kyoaswâ, the last king of the Anawrat'â dynasty, was killed, and according to Colonel Phayre three Shan brothers, emigrant sons of the chief of a small Shan State called Binnakâ, who had served Kyoaswâ as provincial governors, divided the empire between them. I have no idea where Binnakâ was. Pallegoix places the commencement of the Shan kingdom of Siam in A.D. 1,350.

Meanwhile the Mongol dynasty of China had been ousted by the Chinese Mings, the first emperor of which line, an ex-priest, reigned from 1,368 to 1,399. Governor Sü Ki-yü's official Geography informs us that it was during this period that the Burmese first consented to form part of the Empire of

China, and in our own day many of us have seen impressions of the old Ming dynasty seals granted to the *sawbwas* of Northern Theinni, which is evidence in favour of the same kind of seals having also been issued as alleged to Burma. Moreover the Chinese tell us that during the imperial reign 1,403-1,425 a Chinese mission was sent to Burma. But the Burma of those days was only a petty state on a par with Pong, Assam, Pegu, Siam, and Laos, and this point is well illustrated in Colonel Yule's series of maps.

At the same time that the three Shan usurpers were replacing the Anawrat'â dynasty of Pagan, another Shan adventurer from Zimmé (Ts'ing-mai or Kingmai) named Mâgadu established himself at Martaban as king Warêru of Pegu. This Warêru dynasty lasted from 1,287 to 1,540, and had no concern with China, but was at first tributary to Siam (*i.e.* to the *Shan* or *Sciam Yodaya*, meaning "the Shans of Ayuthia)." Meanwhile the Burmese Shan dynasty as distinguished from the Peguan Shan dynasty reigned at Pànya near the modern Mandalay. But before the youngest of the three Shan brothers became sole king, Kyoaswâ, the Pagan puppet, was deposed (1,298); one of the three Shan brothers died; and the third was poisoned by the survivor Thihathu.

Colonel Phayre's account and the Mongol account may be said to agree here. Colonel Phayre says :—" The " deposed king Kyoaswâ, or his son the titular king, " made complaint to the Emperor of China that he, " his tributary, had been deposed. A Mongol army " arrived at Myinsaing (near Pânyâ) to restore the " king (A.D. 1,300)." The Mongol account says :— " In the year 1,297 the Burmese king sent his son " to the court (of Kublai's successor) with an offer to " pay annual tribute of silver, stuffs, elephants, and " grain. For this he received a patent as king of " Burma (Mien)." The names of the king and his son are unrecognisable in Chinese dress, but something like Sinhopadi seems to stand for the son's name, evidently, like tne *shunando* of earlier times, being a title rather than a name ; and most probably the corrupted Burmese form *Thinapadi* of the Sanskrit word *Senapati* or " general." The different versions of the Mongol history are a little confused about dates, but in either 1,298 or 1,300 " the king was murdered " by his younger brother Asankoye, and the Emperor sent an army of over 12,000 men to demand " explanations." Probably, as Colonel Phayre's account would seem to suggest, one event took place " in 1,298 and the other in 1,300. The Mongol " account continues :—" In the autumn, Asankoye's "younger brother Chêsu and others to the num-"ber of 90 sent local productions to court. A "month later Asankiya and his brothers appeared "at the frontier gate, and acknowledged the crime "of having killed their lord. The troops marching "on Mien were then stopped." Colonel Phayre's account says that on the arrival of the Mongol army at Myinsaing, "the three Shan brothers determined "to end all disputes by putting the rightful king to "death. This they did, and, shewing his head to "the Mongol general, said that no claimant to the "throne remained. They then made him valuable "presents, in return for which the general withdrew "from the country." The laconic Mongol account is strikingly similar :—"Now, the Civil Councillor with "the Pacificator Chagan Bukha had already surroun-"ded the city, and the food and fuel were exhaus-"ted. The Burmese were just on the point of capi-"tulating when these two individuals accepted a "heavy bribe to withdraw their troops, the pretext "being that the climate was hot and malarious. "Decree. 'Let them be executed'." Colonel Phayre again shews a preference for Marco Polo, and assumes that the date must be wrong because Polo left China in 1,292, and because he describes a march of "gleemen and jugglers," which Colonel

Phayre thinks) *probably* alludes to this second expedition. There is no real foundation for this assumption of error. The Chinese and Burmese accounts agree perfectly, and Colonel Phayre's surmise is superfluous.

Now, who was Asankoye? It is perfectly plain that this is Colonel Phayre's Athengkharâ, the eldest of the three Shan brothers. And who was Asankiya? Evidently Colonel Phayre's Athengkharâ Tsau-Ywon, son of the third Shan brother Thihathu, who reigned at Sagaing contemporaneously with his father still reigning at Pânyâ. Both dynasties, or both branches of the same dynasty, were dethroned by their relative Thadomengbya, the founder of Ava in 1,364, and grandson of Athengkhayâ Tsau-ywon's wife. Chêsu is of course Thihathu, or, as it would sound to the Chinese, *Chiasu*, the Chinese character used being still pronounced *chia*, *cha* in some dialects, and the faint Burmese aspirate escaping the attention of the Chinese, who only use a guttural aspirate as an initial letter. Thus we find that the whole story of Burma's doings in the 14th century is vouched for by the tallying of both histories in all the main details.

The Shan or Thai race was thus in the 13th

century supreme in Siam, and nearly all over Burma, except in Taungu, whither a large number of discontented Burmans took refuge. The northernmost Shan States were at the same time, at least nominally, under the overrule of the Mongols of China. A short paragraph in the History of the Chinese Ming dynasty (which succeeded the Mongol dynasty in 1,368) says that the Mongols "appointed "Comforters of Pangya and other places in 1,338 but "withdrew them in 1,342." Doubtless this means that both the Pânyâ and Sagaing houses accepted Mongol vassal titles for a short period. Meantime what Colonel Phayre calls the "Mao Shans from Mogaung" carried war into the Pânyâ dominions, and carried off the king (1,364). Colonel Phayre also quotes from the "Shan Chronicle discovered by Pem-"berton at Manipur in 1835" an event "not noticed "in Burmese history. About 1,332 a dispute arose bet-"ween the King of Pong—so the chief of Mogaung is "termed—and the Governor of Yünnan. A Chinese "or Mongol army invaded the country, and, after a "struggle of two years, the capital of Mogaung was "taken. The king Sungamphâ fled to Sagaing, and "on demand was surrendered to the Emperor of "China. The sons of Sungamphâ succeeded to "their father's kingdom." Here, again, we shall be able to show that Colonel Phayre has been misled by placing too much faith in the Shan Chronicles. Not only does Burmese history not mention any such event at that date, but the Mongol history fails to mention it too: though as we have seen the Mongols had officers stationed in Burma between 1,338 and 1,342. The fact is the Manipur chronicle is exactly a century wrong, and the whole story belongs to the period 1432-1450. "Sungamphâ, King of Mogaung" was really Sz-jên-fah, *sawbwa* of Luh-ch'wan. The Chinese Annals of Momein give the whole story most intelligibly. He attacked the *sawbwa*ships of Nantien, Kan-ngai, Momein, and Lukiang in consequence of the Chinese Ming Emperor having first deprived him of his Chinese vassal title for improperly fighting with Muh-pang (North Theinni), and having next placed Luh-ch'wan under the chief of Mêng-yang (to which probably Mêng-kung or Mogaung then as afterwards formed an appendage). Sz-jên-fah (*i. e.* the *Phra* Sz-jèn) thereupon took possession of Mêng-yang. He apologised in 1,442, but the Chinese declined to compromise, and demanded his extradition from Burma. This was granted, in exchange for the promise that Mêng-yang should be given to Burma. In 1,454 his son Sz-ki-*fah*, or the *Phra* Sz-ki, together with his family, was also surrendered to the Chinese. Another son, the youngest, meanwhile ruled at Mêng-yang, and a third son Sz-puh-*fah* was good-naturedly allowed by the Chinese also to live there unmolested. The family came to an end politically with Sz-ming-*fah*, (Sz-jên-*fah's* grandson) in 1,468. He was interned in North China.

A few pages back I have already shewn that the Pong State of the Manipur chronicle was more probably Luh-ch'wan than Muh-pang although Muh-pang or Muong-pang is to the ear the more suggestive name. Luh-ch'wan, however, is a purely Chinese designation, and it is quite possible that it, as well as what the Chinese call Muh-pang, was included in the region called Pong by the Manipur Shans. At any rate the boundaries of the then Shan States were bewildering and kaleidoscopic in their changes. *Su-ngam* is plainly Sz-jên, the character *jên* having still the power *nyêm* or *ngiang* in certain Chinese dialects. That *fah* means *phra* is plain, firstly because the Momein Annals speak elsewhere of a Shan *sawbwa* arrogating to himself the title of *fah*, and secondly because other Chinese books speak of Sz-jên, Sz-ki, and Sz-puh without adding the syllable *fah* at all. Finally, Colonel Phayre tells the same story over again from the Burmese history under date 1,444, where Sz-jên is called "Tho-ngan-bwa, Sawbwa of Mogaung," and remarks in a note:—"The circumstances here recorded have some resemblance to the events of A. D. 1332-33."

To recapitulate, then, we have the following position. Neither the Mongol, the Chinese, nor the Burmese Chronicles mention any such event in the 14th century. The Chinese and the Burmese chronicles both mention one and the same event in the 15th century, and both say that Sz-jên-*fah* or Thonganbwa was, by conquest or otherwise, *sawbwa* of Mogaung, which is therefore quite consistent with his being *sawbwa* of Pong too. The only authority for the event being in the 14th century is the Manipur chronicle, and even that says that Sungamphâ was *sawbwa* of Mogaung as well as of Pong. We may therefore safely reject the Manipur dates.——Now the Chinese were at war with Sz-jên of Luh-ch'wan because he was at war with Muh-pang; consequently it follows that Luh-ch'wan and Muh-pang at that time were politically different states, and that Sz-jên was certainly not *sawbwa* of Muh-pang. Hence the Pong state must have been what the Chinese then called Luh-ch'wan, which once included the modern Maingmaw or Mêng-mao; and the "Mao

Shans" of which Colonel Phayre speaks are probably a racial rather than a political expression for the inhabitants of modern Maingmaw, whilst we can but conjecture that the descriptive word "Pong" was applied to those Shans of Luh-ch'wan who were not Mao Shans, and that possibly the same Pong Shans gave their name to Theinni or Muh-pang, which may or may not have been at some time part of one and the same Shan State with Mogaung and Luh-ch'wan, either or both, alone or with others.

CHAPTER V.

THE KINGDOM OF AVA.

Now we come to the kingdom of Ava. The new capital of Thodomengbya, Ava, and the quite modern Amarapura and Mandalay are all placed in a line along a bend of the river opposite Sagaing, and all four cities are within a few miles of old Pânyâ and Myinsaing. The best illustration of their respective positions can be obtained from Colonel Yule's map, where the future Mandalay figures as Madé-ywa or "Madé village." The thirteenth king of this Ava line was, according to Colonel Phayre, "Tho-han-bwa son of Tsa-lun the Shan chief of "Mo-hnyin," who reigned from 1,527 to 1,543, when he was succeeded by "Khun-mhaing-ngai, Shan "chief of Un-boung," a personage and a state I have not been able to identify in the least. Now Mo-hnyin is Mêng-yang, and the Chinese history of that state says that "about 1,522 Sz-lun of Mêng-yang, in "alliance with Muh-pang and Mêng-mih, defeated "the Burmese, killed the Comforter Mang Ki-swei "with his family, and divided up the land." Sz-lun, of course, is Tsa-lun or Salun, the superfluous *t* being a fancy of Anglo-Burmese scholars, who persist in seeing a *t* before every Burmese *s*, aspirated or otherwise. Thus we see that the Shan rulers of Ava were now Chinese officials in a certain sense. In fact the Ming history tells us that "in 1,384 the appointment of Comforter of Mien-"chung was made, and as complaints had been made "by the chieftain Pu-la-lang of attacks by Sz-lun-"*fah*, a mission was sent to expostulate, and both "sides suspended arms." This Sz-lun-*fah* was father of the Sz-jên-*fah* of Luh-ch'wan above mentioned, and not the same person as Sz-lun of Mo-hnyin. Pu-la-lang is suggestive of some such name as Phra Nang, but there is no evidence to shew who he was. It is interesting to note the name Mien-chung or "Central Burma," which shews that the Mien state of those times was, besides being vassal to China, a mere fragment of the old and independent Mien dominions of Anawrat'â. The Burmese king was then Meng-kyi-swâ (according to Colonel Phayre), which is very singular, on account of the resemblance of this name to that of the Chinese king Mang Ki-swei who was killed by the other Sz-lun more than a century later, and who corresponds with Colonel Yule's king Shwe-nan-sheng.

But we must be on our guard, and not allow ourselves to be led astray by mere similarity of sound. Again, the Ming history tells us that "in the year "1,403 Nalot'ah was made Comforter of Mien, so "that now there were two Comforters in Mien, each "sending tribute. Since Pu-la-lang had divided up "his dominions, he had placed his eldest son Nalot'ah "in possession of great Tien, and his second son "Machêsu [?Maha Thihathu] in command of Lesser "Tien. Nalot'ah afterwards took possession of the "whole, but the brothers were admonished to re- "main at peace with one another, so Nalot'ah sent "tribute and apologised." There are no names anything like these in Colonel Phayre's book, so I am driven to suppose that the Shan rulers of Ava had nothing whatever to do with China, and that the two Comforters were simply petty *sawbwas* of the Yünnan frontier, where there are several places called *Tien*, or perhaps Burmese "pretenders" such as we see now hovering about the northern frontier hoping with Chinese assistance to oust the rulers in possession. This is the more likely in that the Burmese king was incessantly engaged in warring with Pegu, and had certainly no time or opportunity to dally with China. The Ming history continues:—"In the year 1,409, a present of "embroidery was sent to Mien. In the year 1,425 "an announcement of the new Emperor's accession "was sent to Mien. In 1,427 Mang-tê-la was made "Comforter. Now the Comforter Sin-kia-sz had lost "his life in a quarrel with Muh-pang(North Theinni); "his following had broken up, and the Burmese had "proclaimed Mang-tê-la as temporary Comforter. "This was approved, and whenever after this they "sent tribute they always wrote Mien-*tien*, and the "word Mien-*chung* appears no more." Here, again, we are on safe ground, for Colonel Phayre tells us that Mengrai Kyoaswâ, son of the Burmese king Meng Khaung "was sent against the chief of Thein-"ni: the origin of the quarrel is not stated (1,412) "the chief was defeated and slain, but his sons shut "themselves up in their fortified city, and called in "the Chinese to help them. The prince attacked the "Chinese army and defeated it." Again, in 1,416 "two Shan chiefs attacked Myedu, which was sub-"ject to Ava. The king sent a force against them, "and they fled to Chinese territory, while their wives "and children were made prisoners. A Chinese army "marched down to Ava and required their release." The only confirmation that I can find of this in Chinese history is the following from the Momein Annals, chapter on Muh-pang:—"In the year 1,409 "the *sawbwa* complained to the Emperor that the "Burmese chieftain was trying to make his people "revolt, and that he dared not go with the renegade: "if a large Chinese auxiliary force were sent, he "vowed to do his best. The Emperor commended "him for his loyalty and officially thanked him, be-"sides sending him handsome presents for his grand-"mother, mother, and wife. In the year 1,412 he took "over twenty Burmese cities, and sent some prisoners "up to Peking." But it seems more probable that part of the story quoted by Colonel Phayre (no authority cited) is apocryphal, including the anecdote of the single combat between a Chinese and a Talaing champion. This is not at all in the Chinese style; the Chinese have too high an opinion of themselves to fight on equal and chivalrous terms with "barbarians," and it is doubtful if a Chinese warrior could at any time have been found to stand up fairly and squarely in a ring without any back door of escape, or that any Chinese army would have kept its faith with "barbarians" and retired loyally on the defeat of their champion. There is very little chivalry in Chinese warfare, and no sentiment whatever.

In compiling this sketch of Burmese political history, I purposely omit all allusion to the wars with

Aracan, Pegu, and Manipur, and also to the struggles with Siam, Zimmé, and the other southerly Shan States, so far as these are conducted without any reference to hina This omission, I submit, in no way affects the history of Burmese development, such as it is, for the whole of Burmese history, as represented in Colonel Phayre's book, consists of two main phases,—the successful struggle of Buddhism with all competing forms of religion; and incessant wars. The history of Europe and even of China exhibits from era to era the progress of art, literature, popular and municipal rights and institutions, maritime and manufacturing enterprise, invention and discovery, court luxury, aristocratic refinement, philosophy, public buildings, histrionic displays, and innumerable other matters of human interest. But the native-ruled Burma of to-day was until we took it precisely the Burma of the T'ang dynasty, unless perhaps retrograded and more corrupt. Houses contain nothing of value, and are themselves mere sheds or barns of the cheapest and frailest description. Beyond a sort of *sarang*, a jacket, and a light turban, property in clothes may be said scarcely to exist, though such clothing as is worn must be conceded to be in perfect taste. Food is of the cheapest, soberest, and grossest description. Furniture and equipments of nearly every description have no existence. All classes bathe frequently, yet there is no real delicacy or refinement of body. It must be admitted that the utmost decency and decorum prevails : there is no eastern country, in fact no western country either, where the private offices of nature are performed with such scrupulous reserve : there is no exception. Roads there are none ; carts are of the coarsest kind : boats are often fancifully and gracefully carved, and as often as not the keel and bottom are made of one huge piece of warped teak ; but the sails are only made to go either straight up or straight down the river : there is no navigators' art, and there is immense waste of material in the construction of even the best sailing craft. Painting as an art is beneath contempt : some skill, however, is shewn in the depicting of elephants : in bas-relief the Burmese exhibit ingenuity. Embroidery and jewelry is coarse and inferior. In wood-carving there is, perhaps, some approach to good taste and artistic development ; and certainly the graceful construction of some of their wooden monastery spires is marvellous. The ruins of Anawrat'â's more solid temple at Pagan are much in the same style as those of Angkor, Quinhon, Ciampa, and other Hindoo-founded states on the Annamese coasts. As

Colonel Yule points out, the Burmese seem remotely incapable of brickwork of any kind, and all the *details* of the Pagan work must have had an Indian origin. As to the *construction*, as to which he is in doubt, I have no hesitation in suggesting the influence of Cambodgia, then the predominant state in the peninsula. Indeed, there is some reason to suspect that Cambodgia and Burma were under the same king at one time, for Crawfurd, quoted by Yule, says that the "king of Cambodia and Arramana" was vanquished in A.D. 1,153 by the armies of Ceylon, and Yule himself shews that Arramana or Yamaniya included most of modern Pegu. In music the Pyu and the modern Burmese seem to have had some reputation with the Chinese, for in A.D. 1,787 as also in about A.D. 787 musicians were sent to the Chinese Court. Though Buddhism has softened the Burmese character, "yet in no country" says Yule "has human life been more recklessly "and cruelly sacrificed," and, again :—"a singularly "small proportion of their children live to maturity." The Burmese of the Kingdom of Ava, like those of to-day and those of earlier times, did little and left little, if anything, for the benefit of mankind in general.

The Chinese accounts say, then, that in A. D. 1,427

Mang-tê-la was made Comforter, having been so proclaimed by the Burmese themselves, and that thereafter, whenever they sent tribute they styled their country Mien*tien* instead of Mien*chung*. This Mang-tê-la corresponds exactly with Colonel Phayre's Mengtarâ, who asserted his claim to the throne of Burma in 1,426 after defeating the chief of Kalè; this chief had been called in by the Queen of Burma to assist in confounding a palace intrigue. Colonel Phayre says that Meng-tarâ was chief of Mo-hnyin, but this is in conflict with Chinese history, which, however, admits that the chief of Mêng-yang had been fighting with Kah-li, (evidently Kalè). In the year 1,433, according to the Chinese annals, Mang-tê-la sent tribute to and received presents from the Emperor. According to Colonel Phayre, Meng-tarâ was succeeded by his son Mengrai Kyoaswâ in 1,439. Chinese history makes no mention of this' but it states that in 1,441 Burma was given a test-tally and a golden tablet, which event is most probably connected with the accession of a new king. In 1,442 a brother called Bureng Narapadi succeeded: he was, according to Colonel Phayre, "constantly "engaged in war with the Northern Shan chiefs, and "particularly with that of Mogaung." This is quite true, except that Mogaung is not mentioned in Chinese history apart from Mêng-yang at so early a date as this. China was at war with Sz-jên-*fah* of Luh-ch'wan (I suppose Pong), who, as I have already stated, had possessed himself of Mêng-yang on account of the Chinese having attempted to dispossess him and place his territory under Mêng-yang. According to the Momein Annals, "in 1,441 Burma was "commanded to move up auxiliary troops on account of Sz-jên-*fah's* rebellion. In 1,442 the "Burmese attacked him, and in the following year "the Chinese general Wang-Ki complained to the Emperor that the Burmese general would not deliver "up Sz-jên-*fah*, in consequence of which a large "Chinese army was ordered to concentrate at Momein. "In the following year Wang Ki encamped on the "river (I suppose the Tapeng), and burnt several "hundred Burmese boats. The Burmese broke in "disorder, and the Chinese also retired." Manifestly this all corresponds with the following extract from Colonel Phayre's book:—"A Chinese army appeared on the frontier. The commander sent a "message requiring tribute, which was refused. The "Chinese then came down to Bhamo, and the king "advanced with his army. The Chinese now ordered that the *sawbwa* of Mogaung, named Thonganbwa, should be surrendered to them. This was re-

"fused, and a battle was fought in which the in-"vaders were defeated." The Chinese account goes on to say:—"After this an envoy was sent to expostu-"late with Burma. In 1,447 the Burmese and Muh-pang "(Theinni) generals delivered up Sz-jên-*fah's* head, to-"gether with the remaining captives." Colonel Phayre's account agrees in the main, but is manifestly less accurate:—"In the following year the Chinese return-"ed in great force and marched down to Ava, renew-"ing their demand that the chief should be surren-"dered. The king suggested to the Chinese general "that he should subdue the chief of Ramethên: "this service having been performed, the Mogaung "chief would have been surrendered, but he took "poison and died. His body was then delivered to "the Chinese, who carried it off." We may reject the portions which relate to the Chinese marching to Ava and then subduing Ramethên, which is far away south in Pegu, if indeed it is not the Yamaniya above mentioned. The marching of a Chinese army to Ramethên is just as improbable as the marching of a Mongol army to Taroup-mau, especially when we reflect that the utmost efforts of the Manchus several centuries later never took them further than Ava. The most that can be conceded in either case is that Chinese officers conducted Shan or other auxiliary forces into Pegu. The Chinese style the Burmese general "Maha-singisula," and state that after the above events he was made Joint Comforter. Colonel Phayre makes Bureng Narapadi his own general. As his title probably included the words Mahârâzâ, it is possible that *Singisula* may be some Pali or Burmese word such as *Thengi-thura,* signifying "generalissimo." Another similar instance occurs in A.D. 1,770, where the Burmese general Mahâ-thihathura seems to be called Chulaki [? Thuragyi] by the Chinese.

Colonel Phayre goes on to say :—"A few years "later the Chinese again marched to attack Mo-hnyin "and Mogaung, but were defeated: the reason of "these attacks is not satisfactorily explained." However, the Chinese inform us that "in 1,451 the "Burmese captured one of the sons of Sz-jên-*fah* and "would not give him up: moreover they allowed "another son to escape back to Mêng-yang; but in "the year 1,454 the Chinese gave them certain ter-"ritory in exchange for the surrender of the young "chief and his family."

Bureng Narapadi's state must have been rather circumscribed, besides being vassal to China, for we are distinctly told in the Chinese Annals that at this period there were eight *süan-wei-shï* or Comforters, —of course holding Chinese seals and warrants: these were the comforters of :—

Mientien	or Burma
Ch'êli	or Kiang-hung (Sib-song Panna)
Muh-pang	or North Theinni
Lao Chwa	or Luang Prabang
Pa-pêh Ta-tien	or Kiang-sen
Great K'ulah*	or probably Korat, stated to be south of Taungu
Luh-ch'wan	or Pong
P'ing-mien Ma-sa	(doubtful)

This quite agrees with Colonel Phayre's statement that "during this period the kingdom of Burma "was involved in constant struggles with the Shan "states in the north, and dwindled in territory and "power until it equalled only one of the inferior of "those states." Up to the death of Bureng Narapadi, therefore, in 1,468, we may say that the Chinese and Burmese accounts exhibit no irreconcilable discrepancies.

* Some persons have attempted to identify the Chinese word *K'ulah* with the Burmese *Kulà* or *Kalá*. i. e. "the Portuguese;" but this is impossible, for no Portuguese appeared in Indo-Chinese waters until A. D. 1,511. *Kalà* means in the first instance a "foreigner (of India)," and Colonel Phayre according to Yule connects it with the *Kúlis* or *Kóls*. Colonel Yule goes further and connects it with *Kalinga* or *Kling*. I do not see much probability in all this.

We are next told by the Chinese Annals that in 1,472 the Burmese applied for certain territory belonging to Mêng-yang, the object being apparently to have free access into China: it will be remembered, too, that this was the consideration for Sz-jên-*fah's* surrender. As the chief of Mêng-yang had committed no new offence, the Chinese were unwilling to deprive him of his territory, and therefore contented themselves with admonishing him that he must always allow the road between China and Burma to remain open. This must have been during the reign of Mahâ-thihathura, who was succeeded in 1,480 by his son Thirithudhamma Râjâ, who again was succeeded in 1,501 by his son Mahârâjâ Dibati. Chinese history has nothing whatever to say of Burma during this period, nor has Colonel Phayre more to say than that things went from bad to worse, and that the Shan chiefs of Myêdu and Mo-hnyin began to threaten the existence of Burma. The Momein Annals tell us that "about the year "1,522 Sz-lun of Mêng-yang, in alliance with Muh-"pang and Mêngmih, routed the Burmese and divi-"ded their territory, killing Mang Ki-swei and his "family." Colonel Phayre's version is:—"In the "north Salun, the chief of Mo-hnyin, pursuing his "aggressive movements, occupied the important pro-

"vince of Tabayîn, the ancient seat of the race from "which the royal family of Burma had sprung. After "several years of desultory warfare, he marched "down and took possession of Sagaing." This was in 1,523. "Two years later," (Colonel Phayre goes on to say), "crossing the river, he laid siege to Ava, "and the king was killed while attempting to "escape. The Mo-hnyin chief had no wish to reign "himself. He placed his son Thohanbwâ on the "throne (1,526) and returned to his own country." The Chinese say nothing of this usurper, either in connection with Mêng-yang or with Burma, but Thohanbwâ must by analogy be some such name as Sz-han-*fah*. "In the year 1,527 the Emperor ordered "a high officer to go and examine into the facts, and "a provincial governor, named Mang Puh-sin, was "placed in charge of Burma. Mang Ki-swei's son "Mang Jwei-t'i had taken refuge in Tung-u, in con-"sequence of which his mother's family and elders "took possession of the land." The Chinese evidently declined to recognize Thohanbwâ, and their account of the flight to Tungu of the legitimatists is supported by the following extract from Colonel Phayre:—"Most of the Burmese nobles and men of "rank fled, some to Prome and most to Taungu, "which had become a refuge for those who were "determined not to submit to Shan domination."

Chinese history has nothing to say either of Thohanbwâ's successor, the "Shan chief of Unboung," or of his son, or of the next usurper, Sagaing Narapadi, whose reign came to an end in 1,554. Nor, strange to say, does Colonel Phayre tell us anything whatever of these personages. Nor is there any clue in his book as to who the "chief of Unboung" was. It sounds a little like Muh-pang, but sound alone is an unsafe guide. It is plain that the fragments of Burma in the hands of these Shan chiefs changed hands every few years in a very inextricable and ravelled way, and that they are not entitled to a serious place in *de jure* history.

CHAPTER VI.

THE TAUNGU EMPERORS OF PEGU.

In some inexplicable way the Chinese now connect Taungu with Burma; they are right in the main, but the process of transformation defies analysis. The death of Thirithudhammâ corresponds in date with that of Mang Ki-swei; the first was killed by Salun and the second by Sz-lun, which two names are manifestly those of one and the same man. Moreover, both accounts state that the Burmese nobles took refuge in Taungu, a city founded by one of Anawrat'â's successors in A.D. 1,190, at a time when the Sittang river had not yet been rendered unnavigable by a bore. Colonel Phayre tells us that Tabeng Shwe-hti, who was of Burmese race, succeeded his father Mengkyînyo as prince of Taungu in 1,530, and that in 1,540 he became Emperor by conquest of Pegu, Burma, &c. On the other hand, the Chinese tell us that Mang Jwei-t'i (or Shwei-t'i) was Mang Ki-swei's son. The syllables Shwei-t'i and Shwe-hti manifestly refer to one and the same person; and as Mangki or Mengkyî *some*thing (whether *swei* or *nyo*) was by either account his father, and by either account of the Burmese race, we are driven to assume that the Chinese did not know the name of Thirithudhammâ at all ; but, knowing that the Burmese ruling family of Ava had fled to Taungu, and that young Shwei-t'i was gradually establishing his power in Pegu as King of Burma after the death of his father(whose predecessor,a usurping Burmese general, had only been a vassal prince of Taungu,) assumed that the rising Shwei-t'i was the rightful successor to the Burmese throne, and that (Mengkyînyo or) Mang Ki-swei his father (who died four years after Thirithudhammâ) was the Burmese king who had been killed by Sz-lun. This explanation in any case is a plausible one, and there is no other. The Chinese say :—" South of Taungu was Kulah (? Korat) on " the sea, the succession to which was being fought " for by brothers. Jwei-t'i managed to compose " them, in gratitude for which they ceded part of " this territory to him and recognized his sovereig- " nity, giving him the appellation of Tala. Jwei-t'i " now proceeded to occupy their land. All the bar- " barians round about were in awe of him." It has been suggested by some as already explained that *Kulah* is the Burmese name so spelt and pronounced *Kalá*, meaning " foreigners "; and as the Portugues e were hovering about the Indo-Chinese coasts at this time there is some colour for the supposition. On the other hand we find a K'ulah State mentioned in Chinese history long before the Portuguese came to the East. Moreover, if the expression *Kulah* meant "Portuguese" or "strangers," the Chinese would certainly have ultimately found it out, just as they found out the meaning of *fuh-lang-ki* or "Franks," and of the Nepaulese word which the Chinese write *p'i-leng,* meaning also "Franks:" but they never did. We must therefore reject the supposition, and take *Kulah* (or *Kulat,* as it is pronounced in Canton) to mean Korat, one of the Siamese provinces, Siam at that time perhaps hardly yet having become an organized homogeneous state. However that may be, when Phaya Tak usurped the Siamese throne 250 years later, Korat, then called *Kao-lieh* or *Ko-let* by the southern Chinese, held out for a long time, so that there is some evidence at least in favour of Korat having had a political individuality of its own. Colonel Phayre tells us that already Mengkyînyo had become so powerful that "his alliance was sought by "the kings of Pegu and Siam;" and that Tabeng Shwe-hti's other name was Meng-*tara,* which corresponds with the Chinese word *tala.* Colonel Phayre also tells us that in A.D. 1,548 Tabeng Shwe-hti led an expedition up to the very walls of Ayuthia. An *Exposé chronologique* of the Cambodgian history presented to me by M. Lemire, French Resident at Tourane, says that in 1,540, under the reign of Prea Chow Maha Chakrapat, the Siamese were at war with the Peguans, whose invasion they repelled. On the whole, therefore, we are justified in saying again that the Chinese, Burmese, and Siamese accounts here all practically agree, and that Tabeng Shwe-hti's first exploits as a conqueror were in Korat.

Chinese history naturally makes no mention of Tabeng Shwe-hti's conquests in the south, in Pegu, Martaban, and Prome; his invasion of Aracan, Siam, &c.; nor is any mention made of the assistance he received from Portuguese gunners. It is not so easy to explain, however, how it comes that Colonel Phayre makes no mention of Shwe-hti's wars in the north. According to Colonel Phayre, the king died in 1,550, but the Chinese seem to keep him alive for twenty or thirty years more, although there is no distinct statement in their annals as to the date of his death. His conquest in 1,562 of the present Chinese Shan States (which had been lost to Burma in 1,300) as mentioned by Yule quoting Burney, was only of a temporary nature, and in recovering them the Chinese claim to have marched up to Ava. But the present Burmese Shan States of Meng-yang, Man-mu, Mêng-mih, and Muh-pang are distinctly admitted by the Chinese to have remained in Burmese hands ever since this time. The Chinese say that, during Shwe-hti's life, his son Mang Ying-li had large armies engaged in the northern states, and the general inference to be drawn from the context is that the son succeeded the father about A.D. 1,582. On the other hand, Colonel Phayre says that Bureng Naung, Shwe-hti's general, was made *ainshemien* or "heir-presumptive" by Shwe-hti, and succeeded him in 1,551, claiming to be his lawful successor. Bureng Naung was succeeded by his son Nanda Bureng in 1,581, and reigned 18 years. Nothing is said in Chinese history either of Mang Ying-li's death or of his successor. Two events which might guide us are mentioned in the Momein Annals:—"In the year 1,573 the Bur-"mese entered Lung-ch'wan (Luh-ch'wan had now "been cut up into Lung-ch'wan, Mêng-mao, &c.) and "ordered the *sawbwas* of Man-mu and Muh-pang to "coöperate against China. The King presumed to "send a Burmese letter on palmyra leaf enclosed in "an ivory box styling himself 'Mangtala Prince "'Lung, Lord of the Golden Throne and White

"'Elephants'," a title which Colonel Yule shews to have been taken by Bureng Naung, *i.e.* Hseng-byu-myâ-yen. Again :—"In the year 1,583 Mang "Ying-li attacked Yung-ch'ang with a host of "100,000 men and many elephants." If Mangtala is still the Mengtara Tabeng Shwe-hti, how comes it that he is alive 22 years after Colonel Phayre's date of his death? On the other hand, if Prince Lung is Prince (Bureng) *Naung*, why is he also styled Mang-tala; and why ten years later, when the succession from father to son had taken place, is he called Mang Ying-li? And how is it, (whichever king be meant) that the Burmese annals make no mention whatever of so important an event as the march on Yung-ch'ang? Possibly Colonel Phayre's statement that in 1,562 Bureng Naung, convinced that China was instigating the states east of Bhamo to attack Momeit, sent an army into the territory watered by the Tapeng river may be connected with this; but the date is 21 years wrong, and the king is the wrong king. Chinese history takes no notice of the assassination of Tabeng Shwe-hti, or of the mysterious "*sawbwa* of Unboung," Khunmaingngè, who was reigning at Ava. In fact, all attempts to completely reconcile Chinese and Burmese history at this point are so far hopeless, and we can only look to further research for better results. Colonel Phayre says that in 1,558 King Bureng Naung received the homage of the country east of Bhamo up to the frontier of China, and the Momein Annals tell us that in 1,560, in consequence of Mang Jwei-t'i having tried to coax the Lung-ch'wan, Kan-ngai, and Nan-tien *sawbwas* to invade China, the Emperor forbade the different tribes to have any intercourse with "the Tala." There is one single instance in which the two histories seem to agree. Colonel Phayre says that "while affairs in "Laos were prospering, another march to Mo-hnyin "and Mogaung had become imperative. Bureng "Naung marched north against the rebellious chiefs, "and the prince of Mo-hnyin was killed, (1,576)." The Chinese account says:—"In the year 1,579 "the Burmese again attacked Mêng-yang. The "*sawbwa*, having no assistance this time, was killed "by the Burmese." Nanda Bureng, son and successor of Bureng Naung, is not so much as mentioned by name by Colonel Phayre except in the list of kings at the end of his book and in a foot note. He was also it appears called Gnâ-su-Dârâgâ, and his reign is described by Colonel Phayre as being that of the Yuva Râjâ, which means "heir," or "Caesar," *i. e.* "second king."

To sum up, all that it is possible to say with certainty of the reigns of the three supreme Kings or Emperors of the Taungu line is that they were all engaged in incessant wars; that they never seem to have come into actual contact with China; that their nomenclature is doubtful; and that, in this particular chapter of history, the Chinese annalists seem to have been misinformed and to go largely by hearsay.

European travellers such as de Cruz and Frederick appear to have been dazzled by the " Brama of Toungoo's " short-lived magnificence, and give what Colonel Yule justly calls "preposterous" accounts of his wealth and power. Ralph Fitch, however, still found things flourishing in 1,586 under Nanda Bureng; but civil strife soon broke out, his own relatives declared war upon him, and by A.D. 1,600 the mushroom empire of Pegu is described by the Jesuit Boves as being a melancholy mass of ruins.

CHAPTER VII.

THE TAUNGU LINE OF BURMESE KINGS.

The Momein Annals tell us that "in the year "A.D. 1,603 Yung Han of Ava and the *sawbwa* of "Muh-pang sent tribute to China. Siam and Têlêng "during consecutive years attacked Burma, and kil-"led the King's eldest son Ku-mang-ki-chwa. From "this time Burma did not venture to attack China. "Still the various tribes adjoining Burma continued "to adhere to her." The use of the word Talaing here disproves Forchhammer's contention, repeated by Gray, and approved by Mr. Eales in his Census Returns, that the term was invented by Alompra. There seems to be little doubt that Yung Han was Ngyaung Ram Meng, or Ngyaung Meng-tarâ, according to Yule the bastard son of Nanda Bureng. Phayre makes him out to be Nanda Bureng's younger brother: he reigned from 1,599 to 1,605 in Ava. It may be mentioned that the family name of Yung as applied by the Chinese is the same as that used 1,500 years previously by Yung Yu, eight centuries previously by Yung K'iang, and two centuries later by Yung Tsih-ya (Aungzeya or Alompra): it is difficult to account for its persistency in Chinese records, except on some such hypothesis as that advanced in an early part of this little book. Probably it appears and reappears much in the same way as does the mysterious Burmese word *Udi* applied to all Chinese emperors, and which is evidently derived from Wu Ti, the celebrated "conquering emperor" of the Han dynasty, whose fame probably first of Chinese heroes reached the ill-known Yünnan frontier: the name Wu Ti is also given in China to the founders of several other Chinese dynasties. The attacks of Siam and Talaing evidently refer to the intrigues of which King Byanarît of Siam (Prea Naret) and the Portuguese adventurer Philip de Brito were then the centre. The allusion to the king's eldest son is not at all understood, as, according to Colonel Phayre, the king "was succeeded in A. D. 1,605 by his son Mahâ Dhammâ Râjâ." Perhaps he had several sons. As to the various tribes adhering to Burma, Colonel Phayre admits that Mahâ Dhammâ Râjâ consolidated his power in the northern Shan states, and Yule says that the dominance of Ava over the lower provinces dates from this time. The Chinese annals tell us that "the Burmese did "not send tribute after A.D.1,628,"—the year in which the last Ming emperor's reign began. (The Emperor K'ien-lung two centuries later even says A.D. 1,586). Towards the end of this reign, the last of the fugitive Ming princes took refuge in Burma, and the *sawbwa* of Man-mu or old Bhamo, who was then as always afterwards (except for a year or two during the Manchu war) vassal to Burma, took charge of the negotiations. Wu San-kwei, Satrap of the West, and the Manchu Marshal Aisinga marched an army by way of Thibaw up to the walls of Ava in February 1,662, and secured his surrender. This quite agrees with Colonel Phayre's statement that the prince "addressed the chief of Bhamo, saying he desired to "take refuge in Burma." It is not, I think, correct to say with Colonel Phayre that the Ming prince was after his surrender by the Burmese in A.D. February 1,662 [not 1,661,] taken to Peking and put to death by strangling: he himself died of a carbuncle, and his son was forced to commit suicide or was executed at Yünnan Fu; but at this moment I cannot lay my hands on the exact authority. This year the Chinese say that "Mang Mêng [elsewhere called "Mang Mêng-pêh] murdered his eldest brother and "usurped the Burmese throne." This accords with Colonel Phayre's Burmese account:—"The king's "brother took possession of the palace (1,661), "and the king was sent away and drowned in the "Chindwin river." ' olonel Phayre adds:—"The "prince followed up the Chinese, and by the end of "the year they had been driven out of the country," a Burmese statement not confirmed by the Chinese, and not likely to be more true than the analogous statement made 160 years later that the English were "compassionately allowed to depart" after the Yandabu treaty. The apparent discrepancy of one year in dates is owing to the Emperor K'ang-hi having actually commenced his reign during the last titular year of his father's reign, and to the first year of his own reign beginning in February 1,662. It is thought by the (hinese that the *Kwei-kia* or "Kwei-people", as the Chinese afterward called the Gwè Shans of Madura, were so styled because they were the descendants of this fugitive Ming Prince, one of whose titles was "Prin:e of Kwei." There is some colour for this suggestion, as over 10,000 persons, being soldiers and their families, surrendered with one of the prince's Chinese generals named Pêh Wên-süan to another Chinese general named Ma Ning whom the satrap had sent in pursuit of him and his army. From this time to about 1,750, the very name of Burma seems to have been almost forgotten in China, the rulers of which country were amply occupied in consolidating the newly conquered Manchu dominion. In fact the only allusion to Burmese affairs is in connection with the silver mines of Mao-lung, described as being in what we usually now term the Wa or Lawa territory of the Mu-hsö tribes. It appears that for 100 years back a very large number of Chinese had gone there to mine, and the far-sighted Emperor K'ien-lung expressed his fears that there might be trouble in consequence.

The energy of the Burmese monarchs gradually declined. As Colonel Phayre says:—" The reign of " the next king Hsengpyusheng lasted thirty-five " years [from 1,678 to 1,733,] and is only remarkable " for the further decline of the monarchy. A Burmese " force which had been sent to occupy Zimmé was " driven out." This accords with the Chinese statement:—" In the year 1,729 Burma was at war with "Chêng-mai, [elsewhere written King-mai and Ts'ing-" mai], and begged permission to send tribute, but " never did so." But Colonel Phayre's list of kings at the end of his book gives two monarchs, Hsengpyusheng and his father, for this thirty-five year period. However, that is a mere detail, not affecting the general purpose of this chapter. The last of the Taungu dynasty was Mahâ Dhamma Râjâ Dibati, under whose inglorious reign a rising broke out in Pegu. An ex-monk of Shan race was elected king with the title of Mengtarâ Buddha Kèthi in 1,740, and during his time the usual struggles with Siam' Zimmé, &c., went on. For some superstitious reason or other he suddenly abdicated and left his kingdom in 1,746, as Colonel Phayre says, "wandering through " Laos and Cochin-China and entering China." The next allusion to Burma found in the Chinese annals is this:—"In 1,750 Mang-ta-la sent as tribute some " gold and silver ornaments, and presented a com- " plimentary address, golden pagoda, tame elephant, " Burmese cloths, &c. A decree commended him, " and a banquet was given to his envoy in accord- " ance with the rules followed in the cases of the " envoys of tributary kings generally." The Shan king was succeeded by one of his officers called Binya Dâlâ, and it is perhaps to this man that Chinese account refers. Binya Dâlâ gave out publicly that it was his intention to re-establish the Empire of Bureng Naung, and allied himself with the Gwé Shans of Madarâ (near Ava) with a view of extending his conquests from Prome and Taungu over Burma. Colonel Phayre says:—" The king of Burma had sent envoys to the " Emperor of China, representing the great danger "which then threatened his kingdom, and asking for "support. In reply to his appeal two Chinese and "Manchu officers arrived at capital with an escort of "one hundred horsemen and a thousand foot. They "suggested that an attack should be made on the "Talaing stockade at Madarâ. This was done, and "as it failed, the Chinese officers retired without "making any promise of assistance." It seems doubtful whether Mang-ta-la was the wanderer in China, or Binya Dâla, or the Mahâ Dhammâ Râjâ Dibati who was being attacked by Binya Dâlâ: but a place called Ma-ta-la near Ava is mentioned by the Chinese Emperor in 1,767 as being entered on his maps of Burma so as to appear somewhere near Ava; from which we may infer that the Chinese must have had some cognizance of the doings at that place in 1,750. On the whole we may assume that Mang-ta-la was Dibati, for the Momein Annals tell us with shame that in 1,754 Sŏh-kang Jwei-tung son of king Ta-la who had been killed by the Talaings, sought refuge in Chinese territory and was meanly driven back. In the summer of 1,751 another tribute mission arrived from Burma, and the Emperor in his decree expressly states that "the Burmese have never "sent tribute since the middle of the sixteenth cen-"tury [Christian era]. But, when our Manchu dy-

"nasty first established itself, they were able to ex-
"hibit their devoted loyalty by surrendering the "fugitive prince of the expiring Ming dynasty." This confession partly explains the fact, adverted to above, that during the Taungu dynasty of Burmese kings the Chinese were totally ignorant of what was really going on, and confused one man's name with the other.

CHAPTER VIII.

THE MANCHUS AND THE MOZZOBO DYNASTY OF ALAUNG-P'AYA-GYI OR THE GREAT ALOMPRA.

K'ien-lung, * the fourth of the Manchu Emperors, was one of the shrewdest and strongest rulers in the history of the world, and certainly, taken all round, the most capable monarch that ever occupied the Chinese throne : his bright and joyous energy had already marked him out when a mere child in the mind of his venerated grandfather K'ang-hi*—a man of perhaps purer character, but not of such marvellous sagacity as K'ien-lung—as an appropriate successor in due time to the "Great Inheritance" bequeathed by Shun-chï* ; and this choice was loyally carried out by the intermediate ruler Yung-Chêng* his father. He began by promising to abdicate if he should reign full sixty years. From the moment he succeeded in 1,735 to his abdication in 1,796, he

* These names are not personal to the Emperors, but are mere reign styles, such as the papal Pius, Leo, or Benedict. The Emperor's real name is tabooed, as is also "Burman Custom" with their kings ; but the Chinese Emperor affected to insist upon the Burmese kings always naming themselves in his letters, and in speaking of them the Chinese use what they suppose to be the family and personal names ; thus Mêng Yün (Maung Waing) and Mêng K'êng (Maung Khin), for Hseng-byu-Sheng and Tharawaddy.

guided the helm of state entirely with his own hand: he was never ill, and was just as lucid and vigorous at the age of 85 as at 25. His vivacious intelligence was displayed in all departments: his sons, his women, and the eunuchs of his palace were manoeuvred as firmly, as adroitly, and justly as the tributary kings on the remote frontiers. He was as patient and magnanimous in dealing with offences affecting his personal individuality and even with libels on himself as a man, as he was terrible and unrelenting in the punishment of official cowardice and corruption. His chief feature was his capacity for exposing humbug and going to the bottom of everything: for instance, perceiving that commentators for ages had been arguing learnedly about the muddiness or clearness of certain two rivers mentioned by Confucius in the "Book of Odes," he ordered the governor-general of Kansuh to proceed in person to the sources of both rivers—somewhere in the Mongolian deserts—and to follow them both down until it was seen which really was entitled to be called the muddy one at the place of junction. But the absorbingly interesting characteristics of this remarkable man cannot appropriately be discussed further here. Suffice it to say that his splendid career had one jaundiced spot in it, and that was the utter failure of his Burmese campaigns, in which he himself admits the loss of twenty thousand men, and as to which he tells his would-be flatterers that he confesses his disappointment and his mortification. It cost him several millions sterling and the flower of his generals; moreover, as the official Momein Annals tell us with a sigh, the Han-lung Kwan and the T'ien-ma Kwan, two of the eight frontier gates established in A. D. 1,594 as a protect in against the Burmese, fell into and have since remained in Burmese hands. Any results achieved were entirely the work of the Manchu, Solon, and Eleuth Tartars; the Emperor incessantly bewails the abject cowardice of his Chinese troops. This disappointment was partially remedied in the sequel by his own sagacious diplomacy, as the following sketch will shew.

In 1,752 the Yünnan Viceroy reported the existence of civil war in Burma and the usurpation of the Alompra dynasty of Mozzobo. The origin of the civil war is stated to be the conduct of the Gwè Shan *sawbwa*, who, declining to recognize Alompra, had taken refuge in the Chinese-protected state of Mêng-lien (Maing-lin-gyi), and had got to mutual squabbling and murdering with his hosts. The *sawbwa* of

Mêng-kên or "the country of the Kön" (the Ghon of McLeod) took part against China in the quarrel and made himself very disagreeable. On the other hand the *sawbwa* of Muh-pang (North Theinni) arranged with China to murder the Burmese *sitké* or resident, and to join the Chinese. The *sawbwa* of Man-mu (Bhamo state) also offered to desert the Burmese in favour of China. In 1,753 a mission from King Mahatsu arrived with presents of tame elephants and golden pagodas. It seems doubtful who this was, but in all probability Binya Dâlâ, Alompra, and Mahâ Dhammâ Râjâ were all competing for China's recognition. In 1,754 [Yung Tsih-ya, *i.e.* Aungzeya or Alompra] seems to have addressed letters to China claiming descent from Aung-yu, or Yung-Yu, King of the T'an. This letter does not appear in the Chinese annals, but for the matter of that a letter was also written by him to George III of England which is also missing. I have already pointed out that this genealogical claim is as absurd as the supposition that Alompra knew anything of Aung-yu is preposterous. Still it is remarkable that there should be a continuous chain of Yungs or Aungs recorded in the annals of the Chinese Han, T'ang, and Ming dynasties. War soon broke out with China in consequence of the intestine strife which was disturbing the frontier, during which the Chinese protected state of Ch'êli [i.e. Kiang-hung or the Sib-song Panna] was invaded by Burmese-Shan hordes. The Yünnan Viceroy blundered, lost his head, and committed suicide in despair. His successor proved equally incompetent, and the mart of Bhamo, then as now a Burmese town, had to be evacuated after being rashly surprised and held for a few days by an incompetent Chinese general. The Burmese advanced up to the line of the frontier gates (about corresponding with the positions of the present Meungtien, Mañwyne, Matin, and Namkham upon our maps) and even laid waste the majority of the Chinese Shan *sawbwa*ships. It is incorrect, however, to say that they ever marched into China proper, though they may have threatened to do so. A very distinguished Manchu general named Mingjwei, who had served with great credit in Turkestan, and earned a military dukedom thereby,* now appeared upon the scene, and advanced through Wanting, Lashio, Theinni, Thibaw, and Thonzé to a place called Singaung, only a couple of marches from Ava. The embassy route column under the command of a Manchu general named Ertenge, and manœuvring at Hantet and Kaungtôn,

*No Chinese can under the present dynasty be made a duke : his highest title is marquess ; but there is an exception in favour of the ancient dukes of the Confucian family.

which ought to have coöperated with and reinforced him, failed to do so, in consequence of which Mingjwei found himself short of supplies, and had to retreat by way of Mainglôn and Taungbaing, (the Chinese Ta-shan). His column fought its way back very gallantly against enormous odds, and three-fourths of it arrived safely at Wanting. Mingjwei, whose character was most distinguished throughout, insisted on sharing his soldiers' privations and remained in the rear to protect the retreat, until, covered with wounds, and hotly pursued by the enemy, he hanged or strangled himself under the shelter of a friendly tree before the Burmese could come up with him, and a faithful retainer concealed the body under the leaves of trees until it could be recovered.

Thus perished Mingjwei,* like a noble gentleman and brave soldier that he was, and thus perished also with him his two faithful Manchu brigadier-generals Chalafênga and Kwanyinpao. But he cut off his plaited hair cue first, and sent it by his orderly to the Emperor as a last taken of loyal affection, being connected by affinity with his majesty

* This is the Myinkhunré, (*i.e.* the *Kung-ye.* or "Duke" Ming) of the Burmese. Manchus, like Europeans, usually take the first syllable of their names to du duty as a Chinese family name; thus, Lo Pin-sen, for "Robinson."

through one of the empresses. The standard of Manchu duty is high, and an officer who cannot preserve the emperor's honour is expected to commit suicide. As to the wretch Ertenge, the perspicacious Emperor had already disapproved his appointment to independent command, and had substituted Erkinge, but Erkinge was killed in the unsuccessful assault on Kaungtôn, and Ertenge took over charge as second in command. He was drawn and quartered at Peking.

The above events took place during the winter of 1,767-8, and 6,000 Manchus had formed part of the total force. The Burmese had re-taken the Chinese depôt at Theinni after Mingjwei had pushed on to Thibaw, and as the cowardly Ertenge had retreated into China, the two disengaged divisions of the Burmese army were thus able to harass Mingjwei from both sides. The Manchu quartermaster-general at Theinni committed suicide in due form, but he was certainly not the Emperor's brother as stated by Phayre and Gray. No Manchu prince ever leaves Peking unless it be to worship at the Tombs hard by, or unless it be on tour with the Emperor.

Next year the Manchu generalissimo, Duke Fuhêng, (probably the Burmese Thukhunrè), a relative of the Empress, who had also distinguished himself in the Central Asian campaigns, marched from Momein viâ Kazu to Kacho, crossed the Irrawaddy at Waingmaw, and advanced upon Bhamo by way of Mogaung and Mo-hnyin with a combined force of Manchus and Chinese. The Mogaung *sawbwa* was prevailed upon to join the Chinese. It is not very clear how Fuhêng got from Mo-hnyin to Bhamo, or whether he came into contact with the Burmese force waiting for him at Mawla, but he seems to have turned off suddenly to the east at Mu-lah (? Myohla), somewhere between Mo-hnyin and the Irrawaddy, and to have then joined a column under General Ilet'u, who was sent down the left bank of the river to assist him, and who crossed the Irrawaddy at Hak'an, somewhere near the gorge below Shwegu. A third column advanced upon Bhamo by way of Manwyne, and a combined naval and military attack was made by all these columns at once. Bhamo was taken by storm, but the advancing Chinese dashed themselves for weeks in vain against the obstinate stockades of Kaungtôn, though their artillery was fairly powerful. General Duke Alikun, the Akhunrè of the Burmese, who had been sent to replace Ertenge after Erkinge's death, also lost his life in this second attack on Kaungtôn. The Mogaung march was admittedly a strategical blunder. The original idea had been to march upon Mozzobo (the present Shwebo) and Ava along the right bank, but the numerous rivers which had to be crossed soon shewed that this scheme would be nearly impossible; so Fuhêng, who seems to have been very ignorant of Burmese topography, wasted two months over a futile promenade through Mogaung and Mo-hnyin, the only advantage gained being that the *sawbwas* of those states and their soldiers were unavailable for Burma's defence so long as the Chinese army was there.

The Emperor, alarmed at the enormous losses of his troops through sickness, had already renounced the idea of taking Ava, and even Kaụngtôn, when the Burmese King Hsengpyusheng (the Chinese Mêng Poh) sent unexpected proposals for peace. This was after the Emperor had confidentially instructed Fuhêng to to withdraw his army, and to inform the Burmese that "out of sheer compassion the Emperor had "decided not to annihilate them as they deserved." Fuhêng personally was inclined to go on to the bitter end, but he was overborne by the counsels of his fellow generals, headed by Akwei. He was suffering from dysentery at the time, and therefore perhaps unable to act with his usual vigour. He only reached Peking to die there. The Chinese retreat was so hasty that the negotiations seem to have fallen through out of downright carelessness, and no attempt was made by Akwei to take advantage of the unlooked-for turn which affairs had taken. The Burmese appear to have verbally promised to send a decennial mission of some sort, to restore prisoners, and to apologise for past offences provided that the Chinese would withdraw their armies at once and surrender those Burmese-Shan *sawbwas* (Mogaung, North Theinni, and Man-mu or old Bhamo) who had joined in the Chinese attack. Momeit never actually joined the Chinese. Several months passed, but no tribute or prisoners came as expected. The Emperor ordered the Yünnan authorities to remind Burma of her duty, but to his great disgust this letter crossed another from a Burmese general called by the Chinese Nawrat'â, demanding for the first time, so far as the Emperor and the Viceroy knew, the surrender of the *sawbwas.* Thus it was made accidentally to appear that China's demand was only put forward as a set-off to the Burmese demand, and was not original, and thus it came to pass that each side naturally accused the other of treachery. The only way for the Emperor to bring pressure to bear upon Burma without the trouble, loss, and expense of another campaign, was to strictly prohibit all trading at Bhamo, and especially the import of cotton, which by his express order was not even allowed to come into Canton by the sea route. Desultory haggling went on at intervals for twenty years, the Burmese meanwhile writing insolent letters and retaining the Chinese prisoners, whilst the Chinese retaliated by launching arrogant and abusive fulminations and imprisoning all Burmese messengers. Though the Emperor made the Viceroy write in his own name, and say that he could not presume to represent the Burmese proposals to the Emperor, as a matter of fact the drafts of all letters were prepared under the Emperor's own supervision. This was also the case with the letters addressed by the Canton and Yünnan Viceroys to Annam, Siam, and Laos, all three which states the diplomatic Emperor was attempting to utilise for his own interests. This unsatisfactory state of affairs went on throughout the reigns of Hsengpyusheng and Singgusâ (or Mêng Poh and Chwei-kioh-ya as the Chinese call them). Several times the Chinese thought they had gained their point, and made preparations to receive the Burmese tribute; but it never came to anything, though the Emperor on one occasion admitted that his hand trembled with anxiety on receipt of despatches from the Burmese frontier. At last, in the year 1,788 Alompra's fifth son, usually known as king Bodoaprâ (Maung Waing, the Chinese Mêng Yün) sent back some of the prisoners along with a tribute mission, which was very well received at Jêho on the Tartar steppes where the Emperor was staying for the summer. The Chinese annals, which are very minute in all other details, do not give the text of the king's letter, (the Burmese version of which is probably still at Peking, as the Emperor ordered up all original documents, and had his own staff of interpreters there); but the imperial "commands" in reply, sent to king Bodoaprâ by his returning envoys unmistakably use the haughty language of a sovereign to a vassal. Of course it is impossible to say now, the original "mandate" having probably been destroyed with the Mandalay archives, how far the Burmese understood the Chinese claim to "duty" and "tribute" as expressed in this Chinese letter. Up to this date, however, the voluminous Chinese records say not one word about decennial missions, though it is clear from other passages both Burmese and Chinese that a verbal promise to that effect was made at Kaungtôn. The Manchu general who conducted these negotiations was one Hakwohing, or "General Ha." This is the Kyimintituha of the Burmese, *t'itu* being Chinese for "General," and *kyimin* probably being a corruption of *k'in-ming*, "by imperial command." Generals Balamenhten and San-hlagyi, who were also present, figure in Chinese history as Pu-la Mangt'ang and Chanlaki.

In the year 1,791 the emperor sent some presents to king Bodoaprâ in acknowledgment of certain Chinese prisoners taken from the Siamese and returned to China, and in the year 1,793 a Manchu seal for the *sawbwa* of Man-mu was granted to the Burmese envoy at Peking in lieu of the old Ming seal, which had apparently been taken to China in 1,771 with the refugee *sawbwa* of Man-mu, and which must have been preserved by him as a mark of honour notwithstanding the conquest of Man-mu by Tabeng Shwe-hti or Bureng Naung. The Burmese envoy, whose name was Mêng Kan, would seem to have been himself the *myosa* or titulary of Man-mu. At any rate he explains that he makes the application with the consent of the king of Burma, (who had himself received a seal of investiture as king from China in 1,790), and the Emperor says in reply that the king of Burma need entertain no suspicions, as Man-mu and Muh-pang (North Theinni) will of course continue to be subject to Burma, and that the granting of seals to those two states is but an additional feather in Burma's cap, or in their caps. There is one point to be noted, which is that the Burmese did not return the most important of the Chinese prisoners until the Chinese had returned all the Burmese in captivity, and had accepted their embassy of 1788, and they only applied for investiture in 1790 after the Chinese Viceroy, with the Emperor's approval, had promised them rich rewards if they would go and congratulate the Emperor on his 80th birthday. In other words Chinese "rights" are not based on conquest, but on free will.

In the year 1,795 the Burmese sent a mission to congratulate the emperor K'ienlung on the 60th anniversary of his reign. The Chinese state that tribute was brought, but as England figures as a tribute bearer too, both in 1793 and 1795, we may take it as likely that the Chinese wish was in some degree father to the thought, and that more than one "tribute" nation little wot what a political figure it was supposed by the Manchu emperor to be cutting at Peking. In the year 1,796 the emperor Kiak'ing censured the Viceroy of Yünnan for refusing a Burmese tribute mission on the ground that it was not yet due, adding that, on an occasion like this, (the accession of a new emperor), it was unnecessary to adhere too strictly to the letter (from which we may again infer that at Kaungtôn an understanding of some sort about docennial missions had really been arrived at). The Emperor, however, sent the king some complimentary presents in acknowledgment of his civility.

Colonel Burney, in the Bengal Asiatic Society's Journal for 1837, gives a wonderfully accurate account of the various embassies to China between 1,787 and 1,833, from which it appears that in nearly every instance the Burmese embassies were preceded by bogus embassies purporting to be from the Emperor of China to the king of Burma but in reality got up to deceive both the Emperor and the king by the Yünnan officials. The king seems to have been totally unconscious that he was being "invested" by the Emperor, and the Emperor himself wes evidently hocussed by his own officials in his old age.

In 1,806 a Burmese chief complained to China that the Siamese had attacked Mêng-lien [Mainglingyi], and that the *sawbwa's* seal had been lost. The Emperor declined to have anything to do with the "squabbles of barbarians," but said he was prepared to issue another seal if the old one could not be found.

CHAPTER IX.

CONCLUSION.

We have seen that the Burma of the Pyû was at first under the tutelage of India, subject at times to the fitful military domination of the Shans. After a brief spurt of national glory under Anawrat'â (or Nawrat'â Menzau as he is also called) and his grandson Alungsîthu, the Burma of the Mien fell under the tutelage of China, subject again at times to the occasional military domination of the Shans. A second spurt of patriotic life took place under Tabeng Shwe-t'i, the "Brama king of Pegu", who, though of Burmese race, was a product of Taungu, and was not of the ancient royal Burmese lineage; nor were his successors legitimately born to him. Then followed depopulating wars between Peguans and Burmans, with Siam and the other Shan states, with Aracan, Manipur, etc., during which transition period civilization retrogaded, and Europeans began to intervene. A third spurt was made by the Alompra family: Chinese influence was gradually thrown off under the Emperor Tao-kwang, though it is true complimentary missions were sent in 1811, 1820, 1830, 1833, 1834, and 1843,* and British tutelage took its turn, Like the Chinese, who, with intervals of national dynasties under the families of Han, T'ang, and Ming, have passed half their time under Tartar rule or concurrently with it, so the Burmese, with intervals of glory under the Anawrat'â, Tabeng Shwe-t'i, and Alompra houses, have passed half their time under Shan rule or concurrently with it. The neighbouring Hindoos, Annamese, Cingalese, Cambodgians, etc., have been snuffed out of political existence in common with Burma; and the Shans or Thais,† though weakened by distribution over China, Tonquin, British Burma, etc., are the only one of the competing races in the peninsula which has maintained, under the name we give them of Siamese, an independent political existence to the last.

The history of our own relations with Burma has been so often told that it is unnecessary for me to do more than give a rapid sketch of the Alompra dynasty, just to complete the story.

Conquerors, like pugilists, by their mere presence

*The last mission previous to 1874 seems to have been sent to China in 1856, but I cannot find any official record of it in the Chinese books. China was than in the throes of rebellion, and this mission cannot have reached Peking, which was at last abandoned by the seventh Emperor Hien-fung.

† The Shan word *Thai* is pronounced (where it is not pronounced *Tai*) as beginning with an aspirated T. The Burmese *th* is always as in English, sometimes as in *this*, sometimes as in *thin*.

compel respectful recognition, however undesirable their company many seem to others: thus Alompra, though a "Scourge of God" of the Genghiz type, and a rather vulgar one at that, must be given a prominent place in the world's history, if only by reason of the countries which he devastated. Besides, he was a patriot, and almost annihilated the Peguans; in addition to which he patronised literature, discouraged gaming and drinking, and generally did his best for his own people. He ceded Negrais to us in 1,757; but in 1,759, owing to some to treachery or other, the British residing there were nearly all massacred.

The eldest son Dhamma Râzâ, usually called Naungdawgyi (1,760-3), continued his father's ravagings and devastations in the Shan States. He ceded some land at Bassein to the British.

The second son Maung Lauk, usually called Hsengbyusheng (1763—1776), was successful in his attacks upon Manipur or Kathé (called by the Chinese *Kieh-se*) and Siam, besides holding out to the last against Chinese pretensions, as already related. His own people thought him a good man and a good king, and the British gave him a wide berth.

Maung Ye Hla, usually called Singu-za or

Singu-min (1,776—81), set the example of those family murders which soon became "Burman custom," and was himself in turn murdered by Naungdawgyi's son, Maung Maung (variously called by the Chinese Mêng Ch'ang and Mêng Lu), who only reigned a few days. Neither of these kings seems to have had anything to do with the British.

Maung Waing, fifth son of Alompra, usually called Bodoaprâ, (1,781—1,819), of monkish antecedents, was the next king. He founded the new capital of Amarapura or "Immortopolis", and was successful against Aracan,but not against Siam. His policy towards China was, as we have seen, conciliatory. Owing to complications in Aracan and Chittagong, the Viceroy of India sent three missions to him under Symes and Canning, but all were badly received. Assam and Manipur were both occupied during his reign by the Burmese, whose arrogance now began to sow the seeds of their future fall. For a Burman, Bodoaprâ seems to have been a very passable king, and like his father and brother he patronised literature, most of which in Burma is either mythical or religious.

Mêng-Ki as the Chinese call him, usually known as Bagyidaw (1,819-37), was the grandson of Bodoaprâ. Not satisfied with Manipur and Assam, he invaded Cachar. Modern Burma was at the very acme of her power when she had her first collision with our troops in 1,824. War was declared, Rangoon taken, and the Tenasserim coast ceded to the British, together with Manipur, Assam, and Cachar. As Governor Su Ki-yü puts it :—"The king, to save "himself, consented to make a treaty, ceding the "waste land bordering on the sea as British trading "stations." The king notified his own subjects that he had compassionately allowed us to retire, even paying our expenses,—*i. e.* an indemnity. Bagyidaw, as duly reported by the Yünnan Viceroy to the watchful Emperor of China, became a raving maniac, and was succeeded by his brother Maung Khin, commonly called Tharawaddy (1,837-46). He affected to ignore the treaty of Yandabu, and turned a deaf and obstinate ear to the pleadings of our residents Burney, Benson, and McLeod, whom he treated very unworthily. His character seems to have been ruffianly from first to last, and like his brother he became a madman.

Tharawaddy was succeeded by his son Maung T'aung or the Pagan Min (1,846-53). China's interests in Burma were now so faint that no communications seem to have passed between two countries, unless it be the mission of 1,856, until the suppression of the Yünnan rebellion in 1,874. The king's tyrannical disposition was imitated by his viceroys, and the result was a second war with the British. Rangoon was taken a second time, on this occasion for good, and Pegu was transferred from the Burmese to the British crown by the novel process of a one-sided "notification." As the Chinese say :—" The English "filched the Delta from him, so his subjects deposed "him and set up his brother Mêng Tung (Mendoon) "who removed to Mantêh-ye city (Mandalay)."

Maung Lwin, or the Mendoon Min (1,853-78) is described by Colonel Yule as being the best king the Burmese ever had. Indeed it is quite impossible not to sympathise with him and his efforts to get back Pegu. The history of Phayre's mission is admirably related in the magnificent work of Colonel Sir Henry (then Captain) Yule, who was on the envoy's staff. It has been reproached him that he set up as a monopolist trader; but if he did this, it was only in order to raise a revenue and substitute paid officials in the provinces in place of ravening wolves. In 1,862 and 1,867 commercial treaties were negotiated by Colonels Phayre and Fytche. The account of Sladen's expedition to

Momein in 1,868 is fully narrated by Anderson. In 1,872 the Italians appeared upon the scene.In 1,874-5 Mendoon offered to send a mission to China. The Yün-nan Viceroy in reporting this said that "in consequence "of the late rebellion, no tribute had been sent from "Burma for years past:" he added:—"As the king "does not describe himself in his letter to me by "name and surname, and has made use of much that "is improper in the enumeration of his titles, I re-"quest that a form for his address to the throne may "be sent from Peking for his guidance." The Chi-nese account is published in the *North China Hearld* for 1,875; but as the correspondence is admittedly of Chinese manufacture, it of course does not agree with what the king actually wrote. Still it is evi-dent once more that there was an understanding between Burma and China that decennial missions should be exchanged. The murder of Mr. Margary took place whilst all this was going on, and no doubt contributed indirectly to the final *dénouement*.

Of poor Thibaw (Maung Po gyi, 1,878-1,885) it will suffice to give the Chinese account:—"Licen-"tious, grasping, and cruel, his example was followed "by his lieutenants: he established gaming houses so "as to secure the people's substance, and the Bur-

"mese were reduced to extreme misery. On the "21st day of the 9th noon of the 11th year of Kwang-"sü [the ninth and reigning Manchu Emperor] an "English army crept stealthily up into his dominions "and took away Si-poh with his wife and son; and "thus the country was lost. Alas! Burma from the "Han dynasty until our day has existed for over "1,700 years, and now, by reason of a few years of "tyranny and indiscretion on the part of its monarch, "the country has been obliterated in the twinkling "of an eye." And again:—"In former times when "the chief Mang [Tabeng Shwe-t'i] was at the zenith "of his power, the military discipline was very strict; "heavy rewards were given for victory; death was "the punishment of defeat. But now, neither king "nor ministers know anything of war. On an alarm "given, the people are ordered off with three days' "rations, and as soon as these are eaten up, away "they go in all directions. A slight victory elates "them like so many capering animals, while a defeat "scatters them to the winds like a thunderbolt, their "generals losing all control. Their character in "childish and suspicious. Whenever a new king "succeeds, all the descendants of the last king are "killed off, so as to prevent competition for the throne."

* * * * *

It might be thought that, in treating of Burma and her relations with China, I should have something to say about the stipulated exchange of missions and the disputed frontier questions. It will be at once evident, however, that this is neither the appropriate time nor the proper place for any such discussion.

THE END.